The PRE-FAB Cookbook

with Dish & Flo

Don't sweat it, Pre-fab it!

By Debbie Bishop & Cori Berg

Martha's Got Nothin' On Me
Written by Debbie Bishop and Cori Berg
Illustrations by Debbie Bishop and Rick Tierney
Book design by Debbie Bishop
Edited by: Cori Berg and Barbara Palermo

First printing 2001, Winding Stair Press.
Copyright ©2001 Left Field Productions (Debbie Bishop). All Rights Reserved.
Second printing 2024, Left Field Ink / Angel Gate
Copyright ©2024 Debbie Bishop & Cori Berg. All Rights Reserved.

Characters are copyrights and trademarks of Debbie Bishop
Published by Left Field Ink / Angel Gate.

Inquiries: https://www.debbiebishop.com/contact

This book is dedicated to the parent with six kids
(or one two-year-old),
the stressful job with long hours, the demanding partner
or, *God help you honey* ~ all of the above!

We believe there are two things we must do in life:

Enjoy it

&

Get your hair done once in awhile.

Dish & Flo

Nothing gives me greater pleasure than being able to spend all day watching my favorite flicks by the fire while cooking a cozy four course meal for the family from scratch. The kids make crafts and the hubby shouts instructions to the boys playing sports on TV. Ahh, pure heaven. However, I only had one day last year where I was able to find the time to do that. These days, it seems, even finding time to back holiday cookies is difficult. What's a gal to do?

Fake it, honey.

You know, for years I thought my brother made the best seafood gumbo I've ever tasted. I asked him for the recipe recently and you know what he said? "Go down to the chicken place on the corner and pick up a quart." And I thought I invented "Pre-Fab."

The word comes from those pre-fabricated houses...you know, the ones that are built in a factory, trucked to a lot and put up in a few days. They're usually more affordable than building one individual home because the manufacturer's costs are spread out over several houses. The buyers snazz them up with paint, hardscape and landscaping and make them them their own. I thought if they can make houses that way, we should be able to do the same with food.

Why should we spend all our time cooking? There are so many fabulous pre-fab foods to choose from. We can pick something up from the grocer and doll it up a bit — nobody needs to know we didn't make it from scratch.

I've found that I save money this way, too. I don't know about you, but unless I label leftovers with signs that say "It's okay to eat this until such-and-such a day...REALLY!," they don't get eaten. Even with labels, they don't always get eaten. With pre-fab foods, there is usually less waste, because I can buy in quantities just large enough for the meal — and I don't have to get all of those other ingredients that I may not use.

Flo's an exception. She really does make her meals. She's a wonderful gourmet cook of those delicious old-fashioned foods that we all grew up with. When I showed her my original book she said, "You know...you really ought to put some recipes in it."

So there you have it. The story of how our cookbook came to be. A combination of quick and easy or ready-made dishes and recipes that might take awhile. There are fat-free and fat-full ideas. (No guilt allowed.) You can decide how much effort to put into your meals. But honey, don't work too hard — we all deserve a little pampering now and then.

Dish & Flo

A note from Debbie

When this was first written, Pre-Fab wasn't a thing. They had salad bars in grocery stores, with a few store made dishes, but nothing like they have now. Now, it's wonderful! So many choices.

People used to buy every ingredient, chop and mix into their delicious dishes that took hours to make. Cutting corners was taboo!

So, it gave me so much pleasure when ladies across the country faxed (yes, fax - ask your grandma what that is... It's like the times of rotary phones and Pong. And televisions were so big you could serve a buffet on them.) Anyway, I swear I could hear ladies giggling as they faxed their orders in. When they called, they whispered the title. As if it was naughty chef porn. Love it!

Re-releasing this book now gives us the opportunity to add some bits, juicy recipes and more stories as we go. Disclaimer: If you don't like some of the writings in this book, blame me. I wrote the stories and ad-libs. My sister, Cori, contributed many of the delicious recipes you can thank her for. "Our family loves to entertain," Cori adds, "we learned early on how to whip up tasty party food, stretch dinner for surprise but welcome guests, and decorate for a bash everyone will have fun at!"

"We've also thrown in some recipes that are so easy, even our Dad can make them!" laughs one of the girls, they won't say who.

Dish and Flo are characters I came up with so I could write in a snarky style. They are not Cori and I. They were created in the vision of our grandmothers. Clara was tall with white hair and Flo was short with brown hair. Of course the characters are exaggerated for comic effect, and I named Clara "Dish." In reality, Clara was the gourmet chef and Flo could cook but she mainly directed others to cook for her. Both threw fantastic parties that everyone still remembers fondly.

In writing this book, I will "speak" through the character Dish as it's fun to make up dialog for a cartoon character.

We hope you enjoy our little book and make fun-filled, savory and delicious memories you cherish!

Table of Contents

Rabbit Food -
Chewing is a great way to exercise!

No Kidding — You Want To Cook Breakfast?
Somebody woke up perky

Smoothies -
Toss it in the blender & whirl!
Quick meals that won't ruin your lipstick

Udder Decadence -
This section's bad! Dieters beware!

Kitchen Secrets -
How to make your house smell like you cooked all day
while you unpack dinner and hide the plastic containers

Flo's Corner -
Fabulous recipes from the gourmet herself

How To Stretch Your Meal -
Cozy dinner for four just turned into a party for twelve?
Ah, aren't husbands wonderful?

The Day After
What to do with those leftovers

For The Bod -
Ready to wear recipes. Drive your friends nuts
by looking healthy and well rested

For Dad
The stove is that thing in the kitchen
with the four burners on top

PRE-FAB IT!

Even if you have time, there are plenty of things you can spend your day on, besides cooking *everything* from scratch. Pick up pre-made foods and snazz them up when you get home. Presentation is the key. No one needs to know that you didn't slave all day in the kitchen. Your grocer has everything you need to cook the Pre-fab way. Use the time you save on you!

Deli-Counter

It's cheaper to buy what you want, pre-made, than buying all the ingredients separately and spending time cooking. Especially if you are serving just a few friends. Pre-Fab foods from the deli counter save loads of time and money, not to mention your manicure. Be sure to taste the foods you pick up though. Most delis will give you a small taste of something. Unfortunately, most will eventually catch on to "grazing." You know...trying all the different samples until you're stuffed, grabbing your stomach, letting out a great big "AHHHH! that was gooood!" and walking wthout buying a thing!

Salad Bar

Most grocery stores have a salad bar these days. It's so handy. When you're out of time or cooking for just a few, buy your veggies already cut up. (Tasting here is a no-no. Take my word for it and save yourself the embarrassment of being scolded by a grocery store manager with the deepest blue eyes you've ever seen!) On second thought...

Refrigerated Pasta Section

Fabulous packaged sauces and fresh pastas. Try a new sauce with your favorite fresh noodle. Doll it up by adding more vegetables, clams, chicken or shrimp. Serve with grated Parmesan and Romano cheeses. Top with fresh chopped basil. *Garlic lovers - sprinkle in an extra bit. If you serve it to everybody, no one will notice how pungent you smell.*

Bakery

No need to bake - buy it already done! Order what you need ahead of time or take what they have at the store and jazz it up when you get home. For that Fresh Baked Smell, see the **Kitchen Secrets** section of this bok.

Fruit Salad

Forget chopping all that fruit. The store has marvelous fruit salads already cut up! You can even get a fruit salad made to order! Call the deli! Choose your fruit, serve it in a pretty bowl and garnish with fresh berries or a mint leaf - Or - have them make it in a watermelon basket. When your friends compliment you on your beautiful buffet, just say "thank you!"

Garlic

Why get it all over your hands?
I buy mine by the jar. Crushed garlic packed in water without oil. Check out the produce section. Fresh ginger is also a wonderful flavor enhancer to keep in stock.

Have It Delivered!

Best time saver of all. You can touch up your "do" while you wait for dinner. Order ahead and nuke it (microwave) before your guests arrive.

It's All In The Ambiance

AMBIANCE

Presentation is what makes eating fun.
It also makes the food look better.
Whenever I really screw up a meal, we eat by candlelight.

THEMES

Every holiday has a color. Use it in your meals and accessories.
Be creative! Add some of your personal pizzaz to every occasion.

New Years Day

Anything goes! With the way you probably feel after last night's party,
forget cooking. Scrounge the kitchen for nukeable food.

Valentine's Day

One rose, a red teddy and finger food.
Got kids?
Feed them turkey. It will make them sleepy and you guys can get back to the finger food.

St. Patrick's Day

Everything green. Green dip. Green napkins. Green margarita.
Place a four-leaf clover on your lover's pillow and tell them it's their lucky day!

Easter

Go pastel. Serve everything in baskets lined with colorful napkins.
Arrange Easter grass and jellybeans on your buffet table.
Do your hunt differently this year - put the eggs out and hide the kids.

Mother's Day

Go out.

Memorial Day

Have a blast. Invite the gang over. Bright colors. Big earrings.
Serve zombies and barbque shishkabobs by the pool.
No pool? Try one of those blow-up jobs to liven your bash.

The next day, walk wide-eyed up to your best friend and ask if she remembers what she
did at the party. Then say, "You don't?" Laugh and walk away.

Father's Day

Anything goes with sports. It's funny - men will eat almost anything in front of the
television. Don't spend a lot of time preparing it - they won't notice unless it's wearing a
remote control. Hey, you might try that idea on the hubby.

Independence Day

Red, white and blue fruit salad over pound cake with whipped cream.
Or, break out that red teddy, garnish yourself with blueberries and whipped cream and
let the sparks fly!

Summer Luau

Cut out paper fish. Have the kids color them while you and your significant other
practice the hula - if you know what I mean.

Labor Day

Let someone else cook. Go out for a massage.

First Day of Autumn

Good excuse to wear orange. Decorate your table with some fallen leaves from your yard. (Shake the bugs off) Replace your regular light bulbs with yellow ones for a little cozy ambiance!

Halloween

Be bad! Throw a no-costume party but "forget" to tell that "back-stabber" friend or co-worker not to dress up.

Make black frosted cupcakes with pipe cleaner legs and gummy candy eyes. Decorate with fake spider webs and dramatic lighting. Play spooky music. Keep your decorations away from things that could catch fire though. You don't want to go that realistic.

Make your "friend" that dressed in costume "feel better" by letting them answer the door and give candy to all the trick or treaters. Then you can get back to the party.

I usually just go without makeup on Halloween and scare the heck out of everybody!

Thanksgiving

Relax this year. Order everything prepared from your grocer or fav restaurant. Have your guests bring a dish - most people like to contribute something. Buy a few pumpkins and mums to put around the house and go do your nails. Enjoy the party for a change.

Hanukkah

Go to his mother's. Give her the joy of cooking for the whole family, eight days in a row.

Christmas

One Christmas morning, in a strange city, everything was closed.
We found a forlorn little Christmas tree by the side of the road and took it to our motel.
It didn't have a stand, so we hung it from a light on the ceiling with fishing line.
It made me realize, that it doesn't matter how much or how little you have on this day,
the important thing is spending time with people you care about -
And it helps to have nice neighbors with food.

Wait! Who am I kidding? Pull out all the stops!
Decorate everything that isn't nailed down with bows, fresh greenery, pine cones and lights.
Set a table with enough food for the whole block (pre-fab of course!)
Buy all those cute little candies and pastries for your dessert table.
Decorate your plate rack with fresh cedar and ribbons.
Wear your battery-packed apron with the blinking Christmas lights.
Serve spiced cider fro your crock pot while humming Christmas carols. Add extra rum
to your egg nog and meet that someone special under the mistletoe... "What's that?
The line forms to the left? Goose? No, I don't want a Christmas goose! Hey, watch it!"

New Year's Eve

FAMILY FUN

Throw a slumber party! Dance and play games all night. Decorate with balloons,
streamers and confetti. Make lots of buffet style foods - Sandwich fixin's, crab or spinach
dip, fresh vegetable and fruit trays. Better yet, order a pizza or submarine sandwich.
At midnight, bang pots and pans together as noisemakers (or wake up the kids).

RITZY NEW YEAR'S EVE

Make it a black tie affair.
Note: If you're having guests, it might be an idea to wear more than a black tie.

Cover the ceiling with balloons tied with ribbons. Curl the ends with a dull knife. Use
metallic or colorful streamers and confetti all over the house. Order from a gourmet
store or restaurant and serve buffet style using your best plates and glasses. Offer finger
sandwiches, cheese and cracker tray, smoked salmon, melon balls, champagne and
sparkling cider. Turn the lights down and play music from your favorite decade.

EASY ENTERTAINING TIPS

How much time do you have?

LOTS OF TIME

Pick Your Theme

Choose your colors.
Carry them through, from flowers and linens to guest soaps, towels, and toiletries.

Casual or Formal

Baskets and bowls vs. crystal and silver.
Sometimes it's fun to go nutty. Use tacky, bright colored plastic to serve your food in.
Decorate '60s space-age style like in the *Jetsons*.
Wear your hair like the Big Dipper with a huge flip on one side.
Tip - don't turn your head too fast, you might knock someone over.

Buffet or Sit-down

Buffet style—big flowers. Sit-down dinners—low flower arrangements
—unless of course, you've invited someone you don't really want to see!

Flowers

Have 'em delivered! Or mix and match bouquets from the grocery store.
Tip: Cut the ends off under water, then quickly add them to a vase pre-filled at least
partially with water. The flowers will last longer this way. Adding a bit of crushed
aspirin, vitamin C or sugar to the water will help keep your flowers longer as well.
Unless you're a wiz at flower arranging and enjoy doing it, don't spend a lot of time.
In most cases, less is more—and usually better for the budget.
A few glads in a vase or single flower in different size vases are quite lovely.

Basket Style

Serve your food in baskets lined with linen napkins.
(Use a plate under wet food, of course)
Place the napkins a bit up and over the side so guests can see the pretty colors.
Surround a bowl of dip with veggies or chips. Arrange fresh fruit and/or vegetables in baskets. They're not only attractive, they're delicious! *(The fruit...not the baskets.)*

For fruit, scoop out the center of a melon to serve dip in. For vegetables, use the center of red cabbage or a bell pepper for your dip. Serve your other dry foods in baskets too.
Easy clean up!

Table Motif

Go feminine.
Throw a solid-colored or big patterned tablecloth over your table.
Cover it with a lace one or another tablecloth of a different color.
Gather the ends of the top tablecloth and tie them with a ribbon.
Tuck flowers into each bow.
Add English ivy, jasmine or pine to the bows. Tie up, uh, tie in your theme!

More Table Motif

For a child's party, slip toy characters into the tied ends of your tablecloth.
Decorate your food with toy figurines that your child's friends can take home.

Throw a Mystery Party!

Choose your mystery from a game or create your own. Hide clues inside the dinner napkins and around the table. Solve the mystery during dinner!
Keep the answer handy, though.
When all the eyes at the table turn and look at you for the answer,
it's a good idea to know what it is!

OR - YOU'RE OUT OF TIME, & SOMEONE FORGOT TO RUN THE DISHWASHER!

Purposely Scattered

Serve buffet style.

Use whatever's clean. Different types of bowls and baskets lined with napkins.
Place Gerber daisies or whatever you find at the neighbor's in cups and position them
on your table. Mix up the colors. Alternate your patterns.
Wear two different earring and colorful clothes.
Serve two kinds of dip.
Tell 'em it's a "California thing!"
No one will every know.

Disaster Zone

The babysitter let the kids run wild, the house is a mess
and company is coming for dinner in twenty minutes! What do you do?
Well...
Throw the toys in the closet. Get the living, dining and guest bathroom in order.
Toss the take-out food you brought home in some nice bowls and arrange the table.
Place candles in safe areas or use the faux ones.
Now, go outside and turn the electricity off at the fuse box.
Tell your guests there is a power outage. *(But look! I was able to save dinner!)*

Set the kids up with flashlights, games and coloring books.
They'll have a ball pretending they're camping. No one will see your messy house.
P.S. Fire the babysitter.

PIZZAZ

Colored Lights

Lights are fun to decorate with. Color changes the entire feel of a room.
Yellow lights give it a warm, cozy feeling. Red adds drama. Pink makes us all look
prettier by giving the illusion of a healthy glow. Green and blue are hard to see by, but
can be fun if you don't have a lot of furniture to trip over.

Culture Fun

It's also fun "Cooking with Cultures." You can make a meal that's popular in a certain
country, then decorate your table with colors and flowers from that country.
Search for info on the country of your choice, or just wing it. Make up a culture of your
own. Your guests will most likely enjoy anything you try.

Like the land of Schnarfwitz - where you serve extra napkins because people
are always sneezing at the odor from the cheese factory.
It's where the saying, "Who cut the cheese?" originated.
Of course it had an entirely different meaning in Schnarfwitz.

Party Buffets

Buffet style is about the only way we do parties anymore. The food goes in one place.
Less decorating less clean-up. Plus, people like being able to pick out the foods they
want without the pressure of thinking they have to eat everything on their plate.
Tip - If you're really hungry, strike up a conversation with someone next to the buffet
table. You can scarf down your food and get seconds without anyone *really* noticing.

Baskets and Trucks

Baskets are great to serve in.
After the party you just have to shake out the linens and toss them in the wash.
For kids parties, you can use toy trucks, buckets, and toys to decorate the tables.
The .99 cent and Dollar stores have great, cheap items you can get creative with.
Go nuts!

Caution with Candles

I've learned not to use real candles on a buffet. I'm usually the klutz that almost knocks
them over. And then there's the little matter of fire insurance.
They told me if I used candles they'd have to increase my premiums.
With the amount of hair spray in my "do," they say I'm a fire hazard.

Cheap Decor

Decorating doesn't have to cost a bundle. You'd be surprised at what you can find in
your garden or ...shhhh... on walks. Small ivy or jasmine is wonderful wound around a
plate rack. Little pine branches, juniper and pine cones make a fabu winter display.
Whole vegetables arranged in a basket look great on a table. And, of course, flowers are
nice too. Shake out the spiders though...especially from garden roses.
Nothing says "stale food" more than spider webs.

Be careful not to use flowers or plants that are poisonous.
You don't really want to knock off Aunt Mabel.

Check with your local poison control center if you know the names of the plants you'd
like to use. They should have photos on their website, or just do an online search.
Oleander and Poinsettias are poisonous. Pansies and Violas are not,
unless they've been sprayed with pesticides. If you're not sure, arrange the plants
and flowers in areas where they won't touch or fall into the food.

Or use plastic! Tell your friends you're re-living the '60s!
Whatever you do though, leave those low-rise hip hugger bellbottoms in the closet!
That's really a visual we could do without.

KIDS PARTY IDEAS
Pick Your Theme

Choose party plates and decorations to match your theme.
Have your baker match the cake or cupcakes to your theme.

Cut Up Food

Kids love finger foods. Use cookie cutters to cut sandwiches and quesadillas into shapes.
Or cut them into quarters, triangles or squares. Serve cheese and crackers.
Skewer raisins, bananas and apple chunks on toothpicks for older kids.
Tie food bundles with licorice ropes.

Gummy Bowls

Gummies are a must. They come in all sorts of shapes, sizes and sugar content, to use as garnishes for your recipes. Pour some in a bowl and make it a game for the kids to guess how many gummies are in the bowl. Don't make too many as they will probably take them out one by one and count them, before munching.

Creepy Mud Pie

Chocolate pudding over a crushed cookie crust, gummy candy worms and bugs squished into the pudding. Top with whipped cream. Sprinkle more cookie crumbs on the sides and top for "dirt." Make one big pie or individual servings in paper cups.

Flavored Gelatin

Flavored Gelatin is great for any party. First, pick your gummies, then prepare the appropriate color gelatin. Add the gummies when cool, just before the gelatin sets.

Blue - toss in some shark and fish gummies before the gelatin sets.
Shape waves out of whipped topping, used crushed cookies for sand and top with a couple of action heroes fishing, just for laughs.

Green - almost an gummy shape will do - bugs, flowers, etc.

Yellow - Fruit shaped gummies

Halloween - Orange or purple gelatin with black bats, spiders or white ghost gummies.

Fruit - If you want to go healthy you can nix the gummies and use fruit instead. Some fruit like pineapple will change the consistency of the gelatin so if you add it, use less water than it says on the gelatin package. Chopped apples, bananas, sliced grapes, pear and even grated carrots are tasty in gelatin. Some children can't eat berries until older so know the kids in your crowd to serve the right things. Don't serve nuts.

Quesadillas

Flour or corn tortillas
Grated Cheese

Place tortillas in a baking dish side by side like little tacos. Fill each one with grated cheese and roll them up. Microwave for about one minute or bake in a 350 degree oven until the cheese is melted. (About 3 min).

Option: Cut into fun shapes. Arrange on a platter. Serve warm.

Quick Individual Quesadillas - Sprinkle grated cheese on a tortilla. Place in microwave. Nuke for about 1 minute until the cheese melts. (Don't over cook) Remove and fold in half or roll.

For a party - pre-heat the tortillas in the microwave between 2 or 3 paper

Quick & Easy Marshmellow Treats

3 Tbsp. butter
4 cups mini-marshmellows
6 cups rice cereal

Now, before the kids get home, don't let those buttery hands go to waste! Use them on someone you love!

Melt butter and marshmellows in microwave 2 minute. Stir, then nuke 1 more minute. Add the rice cereal and stir. Spray a 13 x 9 inch pan with low fat cooking spray or smear with butter. Spread the rice mixture into the pan using buttered hands or buttered wax paper. Cool, cut and decorate. Use candy corn, jelly beans, chocolates, red hots, tie like a package with licorice ropes. Shape like little creatures. Add ears, eyes and noses using foods from your kitchen.

TEEN PARTY IDEAS

Food

Keep it simple. Pizza - Cheese and/or pepperoni and cheese. Submarine sandwiches, microwave popcorn, soda or instand cappuccino. Bowl of candy bars.

Pre-teens

Let them bake something. Buy prepared cookie dough and set up everything for decorating - canned frosting, decorative icing tubes, candy toppings, googly eyes. See the baking section of your store. They can eat or take home their creations. Food fights may happen. Be prepared. Wrap the kids in hefty bags with holes cut for their heads and arms.

Teens

Decorate with fashion magazines. Set up your sound system with their music. Let them do makeup, nails, hair and/or some easy crafts. Set up a run way so they can do a fashion show.

Set up the TV or monitor with favorite media. Let the kids make model cars or paper airplanes while they also play video games. Keep tape, pennies and paperclips on hand for airplane repairs. Have contests for distance, height, best design, best modified, etc.

Outdoor activities, hockey rink, batting cages, miniature golf, movies.

Other fun party locations

Local park, beach, pizza parlor, amusement park, water park, burger joint, mall food court, game arcade, slot car raceway, laser tag, skatepark, decked out back yard.

Friend Parties

Invite your friends over for a sleep-over. Give yourselves manicures, facials and hair treatments. Nibble on healthful snacks, pig out on junk food or both!

Stock up on your favorite magazines. Set up tables with bowls of "bod" treatments and manicure sets. (Manicure set: clippers, emery boards, orange sticks, cuticle cream, polish remover, cotton, nail polish.) Tell the gals to bring their own makeup mirror so you can all do yourselves at the same time. Have a few extras though, for stragglers.

Lay towels, wash cloths, and a nail scrubber next to the sink.
Set up hair treatments, shampoo, conditioner, brushes, combs, curlers,
blow dryer, curling iron, and hair products.

After treatments, pass around a basket of scented lotions to complete your body
beautiful session. Relax and gossip over instant cappuccinos
(don't forget to make the coffee machine noise),
topped with whipped cream and sprinkles.
Fresh fruit parfaits with nonfat frozen yougurt or brownies and ice cream
smothered in Kahlua or Bailey's Irish Creme will finish you off.

Stud night

The guys are coming over to play some cards?
All right. Place the table up near the TV so they
can watch the game while they're playing.
Set up the computer for games next to it,
to play when that friend who always takes
too long in deciding which card to
throw down has their turn.

Food - Pretzels, beer, sandwiches, pizza,
nachos, chips, dip, cookies.
Or do a hot pot. BBQ delivery.

Arrange it all and join, or
sneak away to stream Korean rom-coms.

Stud night

ACCESSORIZE

Snazz up those dishes with a little decoration.
Just a bit though. Don't overdo!

Produce

Accessorize your meals with garnishes from the produce section.

Parsley and Mint Leaves

Fabulous garnishes! Always keep a little of each on hand.

Cilantro

A bit spicier than parsley, but very popular.

Lettuce

Line your serving dish with leaf lettuce. Use a variety of colors.

Red Cabbage

With the stem part as the bottom, cut the top off and hollow ou a bowl to serve dip in.
Serve veggies on a platter lined with lettuce leaves

Radish Flowers

I can't make them, but they make a nice garnish.
For a party, order them from your grocer already prepared.
Or, if you want to go crazy and spend the time -
Check out **FLO'S CORNER** for creative ways to slice your vegetables.

Orange Slices

This one even I can do. Slice, twist, lay on a plate.

Twist of Lemon

Same deal as orange slices.

Grapes

A small cluster on the side of a plate looks pretty and tastes good, too.
You can wet the grapes and dip them in sugar for that frosted look.
If you have the kids do this, tell them to use water, not spit.

Those Cute Little Paper Umbrellas

Go crazy! Use them on everything.
Visit a party store and pick up a few fun things to keep around
for those special occasions.

Flowers

Again with the flowers... Flowers are great.
In vases on the table and around the house is a must.
Or get the ones in pots and plant them later.

They have edible flowers at the grocery store, that you can add to any dish.
Don't use flowers from your garden in your food unless you are certain they aren't
poisonous. Remember those little old ladies in that movie that started a garden
of their own by serving arsenic laden tea to lonely gentlemen?
Well, arsenic may have a very nice flower, but it's not the best idea for a garnish.

Accessorize your Kitchen, too!

Just because you don't cook a lot, doesn't mean you can't let people think you do.
Bright colored fruit and vegetables look great displayed on a counter.
After the party, you can use them on you! See our "FOR THE BOD" section.

Dips

DIPS
& HORS D'OEUVRES

Whenever I'm invited to a party, the hostess always asks me to bring the dip. You'd think by now they'd know her name.

Ranch Dip

Ranch Dip mix and 16-oz sour cream. I substitute plain yougurt for sour cream for a dip that's easier to digest. You can also use half yougurt and half sour cream.

Onion Dip

A family favorite. **French Onion Soup and Dip mix** - works best with sour cream. Yougurt is very noticeable with this dip mix *(and not in a good way)*.

Spinach Dip

Spinach or Vegetable Dip Mix - Most of these dip mixes are found in the soup section of the grocery store. Follow directions for spinach dip on the package. Hollow out a round of sourdough bread to make a bread bowl. Save the bread you scoop out and tear it into chunks for dipping. Spoon the mixed dip into the bread bowl and place it on a plate or lined basket. Surround it with your favorite crackers. Serve with a knife for spreading the dip. Place the chunks of bread nearby. Yum!

Bean Dip

1 can of refried beans or vegetarian chili
1 Tbsp. garlic (powdered or fresh crushed)
1/4 cup grated cheese

Option - Spike it with salsa!
note - if you cook this on the stove instead, stir continuously so the bottom doesn't burn.

Pour the beans inot a bowl and stir in the garlic.
Top with cheese.
Microwave on high for 2 minutes, until bubbly.
Garnish with chopped green onion and cilantro.

Salsa

Stores have fabulous fresh prepared salsa without a lot of preservatives. Start with this as your base and add chopped green onion, cilantro and garlic to snazz it up.

4 diced tomatoes
1 small onion (diced)
1/4 cup of chopped cilantro
6 green onions (chopped)
1/2 tsp. crushed garlic
1 jar or container of mild salsa

Mix together. It makes a delicious mild salsa.

If you'd like it hotter, add diced chili peppers. Don't touch your eyes after cutting them, though. You can wash your hands in lemon juice to remove the hot chili pepper oil. Or wear gloves to chop, then toss' em.

Tasting tip: If your salsa makes your ears steam, eat a tortilla chip to cool your mouth off. Bread works too. Drinking water will only make it worse. You can make your hot salsa milder by adding more tomatoes or another jar of prepared mild salsa.

Guacamole

I usually order mine from the taco bar down the street. They even deliver. But if you really want to make yours here's a recipe:

4 avocados
1/2 cup salsa
1/4 cup finely chopped onion
1/2 cup cilantro
Dash of hot sauce
Dash of cumin
1/4 tsp chili powder
Juice from 1 lemon or 1/2 a lemon
Garlic powder (to taste. I add a lot.)

Mix the ingredients together. Season (salt) to taste. Serve chunky - it's less work.

For parties - Double the recipe, except for the lemon juice. The lemon juice just keeps it from turning brown. You don't want your guacamole to taste like lemon.

Tip - If you are making it to serve later, don't mix in the lemon juice. Squeeze it on top and cover with plastic or a lid to keep the guacamole from turning brown. Refrigerate. Stir immediately before serving.

Another way to keep the guacamole from turning brown is to spread a layer of salsa on top or put an avocado pit in the bowl.

Flo's Famous That's Nacho Dip

A must for pot luck's. This one is a meal in itself and serves a crowd - or one teenager.

1lb. ground turkey burger
1 onion
1 cup grated jack cheese
2 Tbsp. hot sauce
1 Tbsp. crushed garlic
17-oz can vegetarian or refried beans
7-oz can green chili salsa
4-oz can diced green chiles
Butter or olive oil

Garnish:
Guacamole
Sour cream
Diced tomatoes
Chopped green onions
Diced black olives

Fry the meat and onions. You can add butter or olive oil to the pan if you'd like. Smear butter or olive oil inside a 13 x 9 inch baking dish. Spread the beans in the pan. Add the meat and onions mixture (after cooking thoroughly). Sprinkle hot sauce over the mixture. Sprinkle green chilis and cheese. Spoon salsa over the top. Cover the pan with foil.

Bake at 400 for 20 to 30 minutes.

Cool about 5 minutes. Spread sour cream, then guacamole over the hot dip. Garnish with diced tomatoes, green onion and black olives. Serve with tortilla chips and salsa.

Darlene's Artichoke Dip

1 cup cream cheese
1 cup mayonaisse
1 4-oz jar of artichoke hearts (drained)
1 round bread loaf

Mix the cream cheese, mayonaisse, and parmesan together. Chop and add artichoke hearts. Hollow out a round loaf of bread. Save the lid and inner bread parts. fill the loaf with dip. Place the lid on top. Wrap in foil and bake at 350 for 45 to 60 minutes.

Serve with crackers and bread.

Vegetarian Nine Layer Dip

Refried beans or vegetarian chili
Grated cheddar cheese
Guacamole
Sour cream
Diced black olives
Tomatoes
Green onions
Cilantro
Salsa

Chop tomatoes, green onions and cilantro.
Spread beans in a large shallow pan
Cover with grated cheese. Nuke on high
for 5 minutes or until it bubbles.

Spread a layer of guacamole on top.
Add a layer of sour cream. Sprinkle
tomatoes, green onions and cilantro.
Top with salsa. Garnish with diced olives.
Serve with tortilla chips or lettuce wraps.

Aunt Dorothy's Deviled Eggs

12 hard boiled eggs
Mustard
Mayonaisse
Salt and Pepper to taste
Paprika
Parsley

After cooking eggs in the shell in hot water
for about 15 minutes, take one out and
hit it gently but enough to break the shell
(or slice the egg in half) to make sure the
egg is fully cooked. You can cook longer if
desired.

Remove the eggs from the shells. Gently
scoop the egg yolks into a bowl. Add about
1 tsp of mustard and enough mayonaisse to
moisten (but not too gooey).
Season with salt and pepper.

Spoon mixture into the center of each egg.
Or spoon into a plastic bag and cut one
corner. Then squeeze the mixture into the
eggs into little poofs.

Sprinkle paprika on top. Garnish your
serving dish with parsley.

Curried Chicken Cheese Ball

2 8-oz pkgs cream cheese softened
1 1/2 cups boiled chopped chicken
1/4 cup chopped celery
1/4 cup chopped onion
1/4 tsp curry powder (or to taste)
1 tsp steak sauce

Mix well. Shape into a ball. Cover with parsley and sliced almonds. Press parsley and almonds gently into the cheese ball.

Serve on a pretty plate with crackers

Ham Rolls

Definitely a popular item. You can add just about anything to the cream cheese filling for an addicting treat. Here are two variations:

Mild Ham Rolls

3 8-oz pkgs cream cheese
1 pkg dry ranch dressing mix
1/3 cup finely minced radish
2 or 3 minced green onions
1 1/2 Tbsp chopped olives
1 pack of 4 x 6 ham slices

Spicy Ham Rolls

1 pack of 4 x 6 ham slices
2 8-oz pkgs cream cheese (softened)
1 can diced green chilis
3 green onions diced
1 1/2 Tbsp chopped black olives
1/2 cup grated cheddar cheese
Hot sauce (to taste)
Seasoned salt or salt substitute

Pick one recipe. Lay the ham slices on a plate or cutting board. Mix the other ingredients together and spread it on the ham slices. Roll each ham slice up longways and chill about 20 minutes. Cut each roll into six 1 inch pieces. Insert toothpick in each to keep it together. Place on a bed of big lettuce leaves. Garnish the ends of the toothpicks with an olive or pimento.

Option: You can use any deli meat that will roll up. Turkey, chicken or beef.

Bruscetta

4 Roma tomatoes in chunks
1 Tbsp crushed garlic
Fresh basil, cut up
1/2 small red onion (diced)
Olive oil to moisten
Champagne vinegar
A dash of balsamic vinegar
Salt & Pepper to taste

Option: Add crumbled mozzarella cheese

Mix tomatoes, garlic, basil and diced onion together. Shake in olive oil (just a little), champagne vinegar and balsamic vinegar. Add salt and pepper. Chill and serve with crackers or dry toast.

Tip: You can substitute apple cider vinegar which is better health-wise. It will change the flavor, but it's still good.

Pack a picnic basket with the usual *use your hands it's more sensual type fare* - bruscetta, crusty bread, grapes, cheese, wine and bottled water. Dash off for an impromptu getaway where you and your fun buddy can watch the sunset for an adventure to keep you smiling for weeks!

Margaret's Cheese Things
Fabulous on a brunch buffet!

12 eggs
3 cups grated cheese
3 Tbsp diced green chilis
Dash of hot sauce
All purpose seasoning (Mrs. Dash)

Beat the eggs. Stir in cheese, chilis, hot sauce and seasoning.

Pour into a greased/buttered baking dish or cookie sheet. Mixture should be less than 1 inch deep.

Bake at 350 for 5 to 10 minutes until firm and golden. Do not brown. Cut into squares and serve.

Ranch Drumettes

24 drumettes (small drumsticks)
             or chicken wings
10-oz pkg of ranch dressing mix
2-oz hot sauce
3 Tbsp vinegar
1 tsp paprika
1/3 cup margarine (melted)

Blend hot sauce, vinegar
and margarine together

Coat chicken in liquid mixture
Dredge them in the dry dressing mix.
Sprinkle with paprika.

Bake at 400 for 10 to 15 minutes.
Turn chicken and bake for another
10 to 15 minutes.
Serve with ranch dip and celery sticks.

Crab Stuffed Mushrooms

Large mushroom caps

Filling:
Crabmeat (drained)
Bread crumbs
Mayonaisse (just enough to moisten)
Diced green onions
Dash of hot sauce
All purpose seasoning (Mrs. Dash)

Option: Sprinkle with parmesan.

Wash well. Remove the stem from each
mushroom.

Mix ingredients together. Spoon mixture
into mushroom caps and place on
ungreased cookie sheet.
Bake at 350 for 12 to 15 minutes.
Serve hot.

Papa's Shrimp Cocktails

Bay shrimp
Cocktail sauce
Diced Celery

Snazz up the cocktail sauce with:
1 tsp horseradish
1/2 tsp dry mustard
2 dashes of black pepper

Option: Add finely diced cilantro to sauce
or a squeeze of fresh lemon juice

Prepare a shrimp cocktail for each guest.
Any type of glass will do as long as it's not
too tall.

If you use special shrimp cocktail glasses,
add crushed ice to the bottom section. Then
place the cocktail glass inside.

Place about 1/4 cup of diced celery to the
cocktail glass. Add shrimp.
Mix cocktail sauce and spoon on shrimp.

Quesadilla Pieces

Flour tortillas
Shredded cheddar cheese
Diced green onions or chilis
Dash of salt

Serve with guacamole and salsa

1) Sprinkle cheese on a tortilla and nuke
until it is melted.

2) Place a tortilla in a pan and sprinkle
cheese. Cover and cook on low until cheese
is melted. (no butter or oil in pan)

3) Do the second option but add butter or
oil to the pan. This makes the tortilla crispy.
Cook until cheese is melted and tortilla is
golden brown.

4) Roll cheese inside tortillas. Place each
rolled tortilla in a baking dish or on a
cookie sheet. Place them close together so
they keep each other closed up. Bake on
350 or 375 until cheese is melted. If you
raise the heat the tortillas will brown a little.

Cut into pieces to serve.

Hold the Phone!

Don't miss out on these incredible "I don't care what's in it I"m eating it anyway" recipes. Check 'em out in the Udder Decadence section!

Chili Cheese Dip

A party favorite
See the Udder Decadence section.

Crab Dip

Oh my gosh!
See the Udder Decadence section.

Meals You Can Make In Less Time Than It Takes To Do Your Hair

MEALS YOU CAN MAKE IN LESS TIME THAN IT TAKES TO DO YOUR HAIR

We know what our priorities are, now don't we?

Low-Fat Chinese Chicken Salad

1 pre-cooked chicken
1 bunch of cilantro (chopped)
Bean sprouts
Lettuce (fresh or packaged)
Green onions (chopped)
Sliced almonds or water chestnuts
Tomato (sliced)
Red cabbage (packaged, shredded)
Sesame seeds

Options: Mandarin oranges, bell pepper, grated carrots, chow mein noodles

In a large bowl, combine lettuce, cilantro, bean sprouts, green onions, tomato, red cabbage and almonds or water chestnuts

Tear the chicken into shreds. (This is really fun after a bad day at work). Arrange the chicken on your salad.

Sprinkle sesame seeds over salad. Serve with seasoned rice vinegar or bottled dressing. For other dressing ideas, see the Rabbit Food section.

Amounts of everything depend on the number of people you are serving. Add more ingredients as needed. Leftovers will stay fresh in the fridge as long as you don't put dressing on them.

I usually rinse off the lettuce and cabbage - just to make sure nobody hitched a ride in the packaging line. *(Mmm! These red spotted things are crunchy!)* Wash your vegetables, even if they come in a package "pre-washed." Rinse them 3 times, then set them on a paper towel to drain a little before using them.

This salad is great with pumpernickel rolls!

Preparation time: About 15 minutes.

The Fifteen Minute Italian

Pasta with Marinara Sauce, Salad & Garlic Bread

Pasta

Your favorite pasta
Water
Your favorite marinara sauce
        (or whatever's available)
A little extra garlic

Spaghetti test - throw a piece of
spaghetti against the refrigerator.
If it sticks, it's done. If it falls off,
cook more and try again.

Shell pasta test - Ask your husband
to try it. Watch his face.

Pour 4 to 5 cups water into a pan.
Bring to boil.

While that's working, open a container
of marinara sauce and pour it into a
sauce pan.

Add a dash or two of garlic.

Cook over medium heat, stirring
occasionally.

Add pasta to boiling water and stir.
Let it cook for a few minutes or until
the pasta is soft throughout.

Drain pasta.
Mix with marinara sauce.
Place in serving bowl and
garnish with parsley and parmesan.

Pasta Without Marinara Sauce

Same as the Fifteen Minute Italian, but instead of marinara sauce, drain the pasta and
throw it back in the pan. Add a little butter, a lot of parmesan cheese, garlic powder and
parsley flakes. Mix together and serve. Option: Add pesto instead of butter. Another
option: Switch to French food, I hear it takes longer.

Garlic Bread

1 loaf of your favorite baked bread.
Butter
2 Tbsp crushed garlic
Parmesan cheese
Parsley flakes

Slice the loaf of bread into about .5 to 1 inch thick slices. Place on a cookie sheet.

Microwave a stick of butter for about 25 seconds or until soft but not runny.

Add 2 tbsp crushed garlic. Minced is okay if that is all they have at the store.

Stir garlic into butter and spread over each slice of bread.

Sprinkle with parmesan cheese and parsley flakes.

Bake at 350 for about 5 minutes or until golden. Don't let the edges turn too brown as it will make the bread tough. You can broil the bread if you are in a hurry but watch it closely. Broil it until the cheese bubbles. Then turn the oven off and remove the bread.

Serve on a plate or in a lined basket.

Salad

1 pre-fab salad
Some type of dressing

options: You can add veggies and/or fruit to snazz up your salad.
Some good things to add are
blueberries or pomegranate seeds
diced apple
green onion
tomatoes
organic corn

Take your salad out of its plastic bag, rinse it thoroughly (I do three rinses), drain it or whizz it in one of those salad spinners - then place it in an attractive serving bowl. Add salad tongs and place on the table.

See the *Rabbit Food* section for salad dressing ideas or use your fav dressing.

Many pre-mixed salads come with dressing. Great. Always rinse the greens and drain.

Wok Chicken

Chicken strips (raw chicken thighs or strips or packaged fajita style strips)
1 Red bell pepper
1 orange or yellow bell pepper
1 sliced yellow onion
3 cloves or 2 Tbsp garlic
1 cup bok choy in 1 inch sections
1/2 cup water chestnuts (drained)
1 cup snow peas
Teriyaki sauce to taste (1 to 3 Tbsp)
Grated or powdered ginger (a pinch)

Total time: about 10 minutes

Slice onion into strips then saute in butter until the onions are carmelized (golden).

Add chicken and bell peppers and cook for another 5 minutes, stirring often. Add a pinch of ginger. Add snow peas, waterchestnuts and bok choy. Continue cooking until these are hot - about 2 minutes. Sprinkle with teriyaki or soy sauce.

Serve.

Variations: Add broccoli, zuccini, yellow squash, carrots or spinach.

Another way to walk a chicken.

Easy Curry Chicken
Toss it in the oven and you're done!

1 package boneless skinless chicken
1/2 cup honey
1/4 cup prepared mustard
1 Tbsp curry powder (or more to taste)
1 Tbsp butter

Prep time: less than 5 minutes

Smear butter on bottom of cooking pan.
Rinse chicken and add to pan.
Mix honey, mustard and curry together.
Pour over chicken.
Cover with foil.

Bake at 375 for 45 to 60 minutes
Serve over cooked rice.

Steamed Fish

2 filets of your favorite fish
Broccoli (1 bunch cut up)
1/2 red onion (sliced)
Garlic (1 chopped clove or 1 tsp)
Zuccini (1 sliced)
Yellow squash (1 sliced)
1 cup water
2 lemons

Pour water into large pan or pot. Add garlic to water. Place vegetable steamer attachment in pan. Add vegetables. Place fish on top. Season with all purpose seasoning or Mrs. Dash. Squeeze 1 lemon over the fish. Cover. Bring water to a boil. Cook for about 5 minutes.

The fish should be even in color and flake when touched with a fork, when done.

Serve over cooked rice.
Garnish with lemon slices and diced parsley.

Total time: About 7 minutes

Pita Pizza

Pita bread
Marinara sauce
Red onion (sliced)
Bell pepper (sliced)
Eggplant (thinly sliced)
Tomato (sliced or diced)
Mozzarella cheese (or your favorite cheese, grated.)
Parmesan cheese (grated)

Options: Use a pre-made pizza crust.

Add other pizza toppings such as mushrooms, meats, olives, green onions, pineapple, cheddar cheese.

Total time: 7-10 minutes

Preheat oven to 400. Spread the marinara sauce on the pita bread. Layer with vegetables. Cover veggies with cheese. Sprinkle parmesan on top.

Bake until cheese melts and begins to bubble. Do not overcook.

Cut into slices and serve.

Cooking option: You can saute the vegetables in butter before adding them to the pizza.

Chicken Dijon

Chicken (1 package, boneless, skinless)
1 onion (sliced)
1 Tbsp mustard
1/4 cup white wine
2 Tbsp capers (optional)
1 or 2 Tbsp butter

Total time: About 7 minutes

Rinse chicken and throw in pan with butter. Saute on medium low heat. Add onion. Turn chicken after 3 minutes. Add mustard and wine.

Simmer for about 10 minutes or until chicken is thoroughly cooked. Large pieces of chicken could take 20 minutes. If you are in a hurry, slice chicken into strips for faster cooking.

Pita Pocket

Pita bread
Mayonaisse or non-fat yougurt
Mustard
Avocado
Lettuce
Tomato
Turkey
diced red or green onions optional

Total time: About 5 minutes

Slice one end of pita bread to open. Spread mayonaisse or yougurt inside. Add other ingredients and serve. Option: cut in half.

Hot Pocket

Pita bread
Zuccini (sliced)
Marinara sauce
Cheese (grated)
Parmesan cheese

Option: Add cooked sliced sausage

Total time: About 5 minutes

Spread marinara sauce inside the pita bread.
Add sliced zucchini and grated cheese.
Sprinkle with all purpose seasoning.
Bake at 350 until cheese melts.
Cut in half.
Sprinkle with parmesan cheese.
Enjoy!

Chicken Salad Sandwich

1 pre-cooked chicken
Finely chopped celery
Cilantro (optional)
Red bell pepper (chopped)
Mayonaisse (just enough to moisten)
1 Tbsp mustard
Dash of curry powder
Dash of celery salt

Option: use chicken salad from
grocery store

Total time: About 7 minutes

Remove skin and bones from chicken. Cut the meat into chunks or cubes. Mix in other ingredients. Spoon the chicken salad on sliced bread and top with another piece of bread. Cut in half.

or -

Grab a bowl of crackers and sit down.

Pre-Fab Pasta
This recipe works best with tri-color pasta

Prepared pasta from the grocer
1 jar of artichoke hearts (drained)
Bell pepper (sliced or diced)
Pesto sauce
cherry tomatoes (sliced in half)
Red onion (Sliced chunky)
1 Tbsp crushed garlic

Total time: About 5 minutes

Heat the pesto in the microwave for about 30 seconds.
Drain the oil from the pesto sauce. (A strainer works well for this)

Dump your pasta in to a pretty bowl
Add the other ingredients. Toss thoroughly. Garnish with a little parmesan cheese.

Option: Heat the whole mixure in the microwave for a minute before serving.

Serve with garlic bread or hot rolls.

Easy Ques-Yourdillas

Tortilla
Grated cheddar cheese
Beans (refried or vegetarian chili)
Red onion (sliced or diced)
Tomatoes (sliced or diced)
Green onion (chopped)
Cilantro (chopped)
Salsa

Total time: Less than 5 minutes

Place a tortilla on a plate. Add beans, veggies and cheese.
Lay another tortilla on top.
Nuke for 1 minute
or
Place in frying pan and cover. Cook in a pan on medium to low heat for about 1 to 2 minutes until cheese is mostly melted and tortilla is slightly browned. Then flip over and brown the other side. You can add butter to the pan or cook it without butter. You can add butter or oil to the pan first if you want a crispier golden brown tortilla.

Tip from Dish: Pre-fab your veggies! Get them from the salad bar or grocer

Tip from Flo: Melt the cheese, but don't let it bubble too much. Overcooked cheese is hard, crusty anf not very appetizing.

Dish: Wow! That party was so long ago. I thought you'd forgotten about it by now.

Flo: Believe me, I've tried.

Yummy Fajita Style Chicken

Grilled chicken strips (see your deli or meat section)
Yellow onion (sliced or diced)
Red bell pepper (sliced or diced)
Yellow bell pepper (sliced or diced)
Orange bell pepper (sliced or diced)
Butter (2-4 Tbsp)

Add butter to frying pan
Add onions and bell peppers to pan
Heat on medium to low depending how rushed you are. Carmelize the onion and peppers mixture - meaning, sautee it until the onions turn slightly brown on the edges...its tasty this way.

You can cook it less, and not carmelize it. It is still delicious, just less savory.

Add the chicken strips. They are pre-cooked so they only have to be heated for a few minutes.

Ways to serve

Eat it as is

Use in tortillas for tacos or fajitas

Fry a flour tortilla in butter with grated cheese and the chicken mix. Fold and add a second one. Cover and cook until cheese is melted. Flip to brown tortilla on the other side. Serve.

Or serve with mashed potatoes or rice.

For a quick ramen style meal, cook rice noodles in chicken broth. Add this mixture as you serve. Top with diced green onions and a soft boiled egg if you'd like.

Soft boiled egg - boil water. Add eggs. Cook 6 min. Dump water. Add cold water and remove eggs from shells. If you slice the egg in half it makes it easier to remove from the shell.

Easy Noodles

Chicken broth
Your favorite noodles
Green onions (diced)

Option: Add soft or hard boiled egg

Pour one or two cartons of chicken or vegetable broth into a pot
Heat until boiling
Add noodles
Lower heat to medium or low and cook until the noodles are done - soft, but not pasty.

Serve noodles and broth in bowls.

Tip from Dish: If you use gluten-free noodles, watch them. If cooked too long those suckers DISAPPEAR!

One Dish And You're Done Dinners

ONE DISH AND YOU'RE DONE DINNERS

All the food groups in one pan! Easy clean-up!

John's Fabulous Macaroni & Cheese

1 package macaroni and cheese
Milk
Mushrooms (sliced)
Broccoli tops
Zuccini (sliced)
Bell pepper (chopped)
Steak or chicken (cooked, cubed)

Saute the veggies and meat together. Set aside. Follow the directions on the macaroni and cheese box. (You can leave out or reduce the butter if you'd like.)

Add the veggies and meat to the macaroni and cheese and cook over medium heat stirring constantly for 2 more minutes.

Serve.

Macaroni and Cheese from scratch
What? Are you kidding? I know, not pre-fab, but delish!

1 package pasta of your choice
1/2 to 1 cup Milk
3 Tbsp Butter
1 cup Cheddar cheese
1/4 cup Parmesan cheese

Option: Add more cheese
Gouda
Smokehouse cheddar
Salt and Pepper to taste

Fill a tall pot with water and bring to boil. Add pasta and cook until done.
Pinch a piece of pasta to see if it is all the same color (done). If the center looks a little different, it isn't done. Cook longer.

Drain water. (use a strainer, and pot holders) Place back on stove. Add milk, butter garlic and cheese. Cook over low heat, stirring gently. Fold in the cheese. Cook until the cheese melts and the mixture is creamy. Add more milk if desired.

To reheat the next day, add more milk or water. You can microwave it to heat, but you should add liquid so it is creamy.

Vegetable Marinara

Zuccini (sliced)
Yellow squash (sliced)
Eggplant (chopped)
Onion (sliced)
Red Bell pepper (chopped)
Orange Bell pepper (chopped)
Parsley (finely chopped)
1 container marinara sauce
1/2 Tbsp crushed garlic
1 to 2 Tbsp Butter
All purpose seasoning
Italian seasoning
Pasta

Saute the veggies in butter for about 2 minutes, stirring occasionally. Add seasoning.
Add marinara sauce
Cook over medium heat until thoroughly bubbly, stirring often.

Serve over any type of cooked pasta.

Option: Spread pesto on any type of bread or bread sticks. Bake at 350 until bread is warmed and slightly golden. Sprinkle with parmesan cheese and a touch of salt.

Vegetable Lasagne

Zuccini (sliced) or Eggplant (sliced)
Onion (chopped)
Bell pepper (chopped)
Spinach (10 oz package frozen spinach)
3 Tbsp crushed garlic

Lasagna noodles (cooked)
Marinara sauce (2 containers or 4 cups)
Ricotta cheese (1 container)

Mozzarella cheese
Parmesan cheese

Option: Add cooked ground turkey meat

Toss the veggie ingredients and garlic into a blender and buzz on medium speed until blended to a course pulp.

Fill a tall pot with water and bring to boil.
Add pasta and cook until done.
Pinch a piece of pasta to see if it is all the same color (done). If the center looks a little different, it isn't done. Cook longer.
Drain water. (use a strainer, and pot holders)

Grease a baking dish with butter. Layer the baking dish with one layer of cooked noodles. Spoon some of the blended veggie mix on the noodles. Add marinara sauce. Add another layer of noodles. Add more vegetable mixture, and more marinara sauce. Add a layer of ricotta cheese. Alternate noodles, marinara and veggie mix. Top with mozzarella cheese and parmesan.

Vegetable Casserole

1 bunch or package broccoli
1 package spinach (frozen, chopped)
1 jar artichoke hearts (drained)
1 package peas (frozen)
1 white or yellow onion (chopped)
2 zuccini or yellow squash (chopped)
1 small can diced green chilis
3 eggs
1 package grated cheddar cheese
2 Tbsp water
All purpose seasoning

Option: Use any vegetables you like

Pre-heat oven to 350. Grease a baking dish.

Rinse and drain the vegetables, then layer them in the baking dish.

Beat the eggs, water, chilis, cheese and seasoning together. Spread the mixture over the vegetables. (I usually poke it with a fork, then sprinkle a little more grated cheese on top.

Bake for 30 minutes. It should be bubbly but not brown.

Rice

I'm not very good with rice. People who eat my rice say, "Mmm...this tastes very healthy." Then they excuse themselves for a few minutes. Take my word for it. If you want to make rice, get the recipe from a different book.

Or better yet - Buy it pre-made (see the frozen foods section of your grocery store). Snazz it up with diced veggies like green onion or parsley. Hide those containers!

Tip from Flo: Get a rice cooker!

Dish: Preferably a cute one.

OK - I'll give you one recipe for rice

1 part rice
2 parts water (or chicken broth)
Dash of salt
automatic rice cooker with lid.

Measure your ingredients.

Rice Cooker - Follow manufacturers directions to measure and cook.

Pan - Touch the tip of your finger to the inside bottom of the pan. Fill rice to the bottom knuckle. Pour water to the top knuckle (where your finger meets your hand.)

Cover. Bring to a boil. I was told not to peek at the rice. It lets the steam out. Wait until the lid starts to jump up and down, then lower the heat to simmer.

I don't know how long you should simmer it. I'm not a great rice cooker. I usually cook it to the the point when the rice sucks up all the water and before the pan burns. Add more water if your rice is still not cooked all the way. It's done when it is not crunchy.

Moisten or flavor it with some type of sauce and serve.

Somebody else's recipe for sushi rice

1 cup rice
2 cups cold water
3 Tbsp sugar
1/4 c rice vinegar
Dash of salt

Combine ingredients in a sauce pan. Bring to a rapid boil. About 5 minutes. Don't open the lid. (See? What'd I tell you?)

Reduce heat to medium and cook for 10 minutes. Reduce heat to low and cook for 15 minutes.

When rice is done, spread it out on a cookie sheet to cool. Heat 3 Tbsp plus tsp of sugar until dissolved. Add 1/4 cup rice vinegar Pour over rice and mix. You are now ready to make sushi!

Sushi

My favorite way to do sushi is to eat out!

My second favorite way is to buy it from the grocery store. Arrange it on a platter. Garnish with the ginger and wasabi that came in the cute little box. Serve low salt soy sauce on the side. Orange slices for dessert. But if you really want to make it, here are a few recipes:

Reiko's Philadelphia Roll

Fabulous hors d'oeuvre!

Cream cheese
Smoked salmon
Thin cucumber strips
Nori seaweed sheets (toasted)
Sushi rice

Option: Add a thin slice of carrot

Lay seaweed on a piece of plastic wrap. Spread rice on seaweed. Layer cream cheese, salmon and cucumber. Use plastic wrap to help roll it up.

Cut into 1 inch pieces. Remove plastic. Arrange on a plate with soy sauce.

Sashimi

**Fresh ahi or high quality tuna
(tell your butcher it's for sashimi)
Low salt soy sauce
Fresh prepared ginger (buy it from the
sushi bar at your grocer)
Wasabi (prepared Japanese horseradish)**

Slice the tuna into 2 inch long 1/4 inch thick strips. Cut at an angle with the grain of the fish. Arrange the strips on a platter.

Place the ginger and wasabi in little mounds on the platter. Garnish with thinly sliced lemons and carrot strips.

Serve with soy sauce and individual dipping bowls.

California Roll

**Crabmeat
Cucumber (sliced lengthwise in quarters)
Avocado (sliced into strips)
Sushi rice
Seaweed**

If you have a sushi roller, cover it with a sheet of plastic wrap or wax paper to keep the rice from squishing out the grooves.

Place the seaweed square on the roller.

Add 1/2 cup rice and flatten it over the surface of the seaweed.

Down the center of the square add crabmeat, avocado and cucumber.

Roll up.

Remove plastic or wax paper and cut into 1 inch pieces.

Serve with soy sauce, wasabi and ginger on the side.

Tip from Flo - Always cover your bamboo sushi roller with plastic wrap (tape to secure) to keep the seaweed from sticking.

Also have a bowl of water handy, dip your fingers in the water before spreading the rice so it won't stick to your hands.

Veggie Roll

Cucumber (sliced lengthwise in quarters)
Avocado (sliced into strips)
carrot (very thin slice - or use the grater)
green onion
Sushi rice
Seaweed

Place the seaweed square on the roller. Add 1/2 cup rice and flatten it over the surface of the seaweed. Down the center of the square add the ingredients. Roll up. Remove plastic or wax paper and cut into 1 inch pieces.

Serve with soy sauce, wasabi and ginger on the side. Add a dish of small slices of apple to cleanse the tastebuds. Refreshing after eating the sushi.

Note: Gala or Honeycrisp apples are good with this. Green apples, although tasty, are a bit sour so the taste clashes with the onion.

Eggplant Parmesan

Eggplant
Mozzarella cheese
Parmesan cheese
Parsley
Good company

Grease a baking pan with butter. Cut the eggplant into 1 inch thick slices.

Layer the eggplant in the baking dish. Cover with marinara sauce. Top with mozzarella cheese. Add another layer if you'd like. Cover with marinara sauce and top with mozzarella cheese.

Bake at 350 for 20 to 30 minutes. Remove from oven. Sprinkle with parmesan cheese. Carnish with chopped parsley. Serve with garlic bread and great music.

One dish option: Add 1 cup of water and 1 cup of rice.

Chicken with Vegetables

1 package chicken (boneless, skinless)
1 potato
1/2 cup fresh green beans
1/2 cup carrots
1/4 cup red onion
1/2 cup yellow zucchini
2 envelopes chicken soup mix*
2/3 cup chicken broth
2 Tbsp butter

*optional seasonings: Poultry seasoning, celery seed, coriander, bouquet garni

Place butter in frying pan on stove. Cut or just add the chicken and brown over medium heat. Stir in sliced vegetables. Add seasonings and chicken broth. Cover and simmer for 45 minutes.

One dish option: Add 1 cup of water and 1 cup of rice.

Quick Frozen Entree

1 frozen entree (your favorite)
1 glass of good wine (also your favorite)

Sip the wine to make sure it's good. Remove the frozen entree from its package and microwave until its done.

Have some more wine. Remove the hot entree from the microwave and peel back the plastic covering. Serve.

Option: Non-alcoholic beverage will do just as well.

Pizza Sandwich

1 loaf of brown & serve french bread
1/2 lb. ground meat
2 Tbsp. grated parmesan cheese
A dash of pepper
2 Tbsp chopped black olives
1 tsp chopped green onion
3 oz tomato paste
Shredded or grated mozzarella cheese

Cut the loaves into halves horizontally. Combine all ingredients except the cheese. Spread 1/2 of the mixture on each loaf of bread.

Place the bread, meat side up, on an ungreased cookie sheet. Bake at 350 for 25 minutes.

Remove from oven. Sprinkle cheese over the top and bake for 5 more minutes. (Or until cheese is melted, but not brown.)

Take out of oven and cut loaves diagonally into individual servings.

Quick Frozen Entree

1 frozen entree (your favorite)
1 glass of good wine (also your favorite)

Sip the wine to make sure it's good. Remove the frozen entree from its package and microwave until its done.

Have some more wine. Remove the hot entree from the microwave and peel back the plastic covering. Serve.

Option: Non-alcoholic beverage will do just as well.

Goulash

One dish, two pans - it's still easy

Lean ground turkey meat
2 cups marinara sauce (1 jar)
1 onion (chopped)
1/2 package frozen corn
1 package pasta shells
Garlic (2 Tbsp crushed or to taste)
All purpose seasoning

Total time about 20 minutes.

In a pot combine water and pasta. Bring to a boil. Cook until pasta is done.

While that's working, saute ground turkey and onions in a large pan. Add marinara sauce, corn and spices. Simmer for about 10 minutes. Mix in the cooked pasta.

Serve with crusty Italian bread or rolls.

Note: This goulash is really good, but the combination of foods might not digest well. To eliminate an after dinner unpleasantries, leave out the meat. Or just enjoy it. Have seconds! If anyone notices a terrible odor coming from your direction, stare at the dog in disgust.

Carne Asada

Thin, top sirloin steak (or ask your butcher what they recommend)
Fresh lime juice
Beer
Garlic
Oregano
Tiny pinch of chili pepper
Dash of soy sauce

Marinate meat in mixture for at least 15 minutes. One hour is better.

Barbque and serve taco style

Option: Serve in a bowl over beans and rice. Garnish with chopped onion, tomato and cilantro. Substitute chicken for beef.

Buy it already made from a nearby store or restaurant. Hide those containers!

Fish on the Rocks

Filets of fish
2 cups rice
Vegetable or chicken broth
1 large onion (chopped)
6 green onions (diced)
4 large tomatoes (diced)
2 Tbsp crushed garlic
1 Tbsp olive oil
1 lemon
6 mushrooms (sliced)
Dash of pepper
Dash of cayenne
1/2 tsp paprika
1/4 cup cilantro (chopped)

Combine the rice and chopped oinions. Spread mixture inside a large baking dish. Lay the fish filets on top. Add broth.

In a bowl, combine tomatoes, garlic, olive oil and seasonings. Set aside.

Place mushrooms and green onions on fish. Squeeze the juice from one lemon over fish. Add cilantro. Spoon 1/2 of the tomato mixture over fish. Sprinkle with paprika.

Cover. Bake at 400 for 30 minutes. Garnish with more tomato mixture and green onion.

Tacos

1 package ground chicken or turkey
1 can fat-free chicken broth
Finely chopped vegetables
    carrots
    green onions
    cilantro
    mushrooms
    tomatoes
    red or orange bell pepper

Cook together over medium heat.

Dash of chili powder
1 Tbsp garlic
1/2 dash of cumin
Dash of water

Saute for 5 more minutes

Serve with tortillas, shredded cheese, shredded lettuce, guacamole and salsa.

Option: Adding cornstarch will reduce the chance of taco meat dripping onto your pants. Mix the cornstarch with cool water, then add it to the meat. Otherwise it will make lumps.

For the tortillas, add oil to pan (I use coconut oil but use what you'd like) cook one side of the tortilla for about 30 seconds and turn over. Fold in half. Brown each side. Drain on paper towel.

Cori's Chicken Enchiladas

Sauce
1 can cream of chicken soup   Mix together over medium heat
1 cup sour cream
Diced green chiles
Dash of Italian seasoning
1 small can of green enchilada sauce
1/8 tsp cumin
Dash of coriander
1-2 cloves minced garlic
Dash of onion powder

Chicken Filling   Boil and shred chicken (or tear apart a pre-
1 chicken   cooked one)

Add   Add to chicken and saute in butter
1/2 cup mushrooms
1/2 cup diced red bell pepper
1/2 cup cilantro
1/2 cup green onion
1 small can diced green chilis

Heat 12 corn tortillas. Dip in sauce then place in baking dish. Add chicken filling and grated jack cheese. Roll and continue until pan is full. Pour remaining sauce over the enchiladas and top with jack cheese. Bake at 375 for 30 minutes until bubbly. Garnish with avocado, salsa, cilantro and fresh diced tomato.

In a hurry? Instead of rolling enchiladas - layer tortillas, chicken, sauce and cheese. Bake. *It all goes to the same place anyway.*

Kitchen Sink Enchiladas

Step 1

1 package chicken strips (boneless, skinless, cut up)
1 yellow or white onion (chopped)
1 orange bell pepper (sliced)
1 red bell pepper (sliced)
Cilantro (1 bunch, chopped)
1 tsp garlic
1/2 tsp cumin
1/2 tsp chili powder
All purpose seasoning

Saute the ingredients together for about 5 minutes (or until the chicken is done)

Step 2

Tortillas (corn or flour)
Grated cheese (jack or cheddar)
Tomato (chopped)
4 green onions (chopped)
Shredded lettuce
Salsa

Spoon the chicken mixture down the center of tortilla, Add cheese, tomato, onions, lettuc and salsa.
Roll up and place on plates

Garnish with a dollop of sour cream and guacamole. Sprinkle more salsa and cilantro on top.

Option: Add 1 or 2 cans of vegetarian chili to chicken mixture. Cook about 30 seconds after bubbly.

Serve with *Flo's Famous "That's Nacho Dip!"* and tortilla chips.

Total time: About 25 minutes.

Provide crane service to move your guests to their cars after dinner.

Stuffed Zucchini

8 large zucchinis
1 eggplant
2 tomatoes
1 bell pepper
1 onion
1 yellow squash
1 tsp crushed garlic
1 tsp all purpose seasoning
Parmesan cheese
1 container marinara sauce
Sliced mozzarella or jack cheese

Step 2
Tortillas (corn or flour)
Grated cheese (jack or cheddar)
Tomato (chopped)
4 green onions (chopped)
Shredded lettuce
Salsa

Slice zucchini horizontally and scoop out the insides being careful not to destroy the outer skin.

Chop other vegetables and toss them in the blender with the scooped out zucchini "meat." Add seasonings. Set blender on chop and turn on. Mixture should be finely chopped and well blended.

Grease a backing dish with olive oil. Place zucchini shells in the baking dish. Spoon mixture into zucchini shells. Cover with marinara sauce. (I like to add a little extra garlic to store bought marinara sauce.) Lay cheese on zucchini and sprinkle with Parmesan.

Bake at 350 for 25 minutes. Serve with hot pumpernickle rolls.

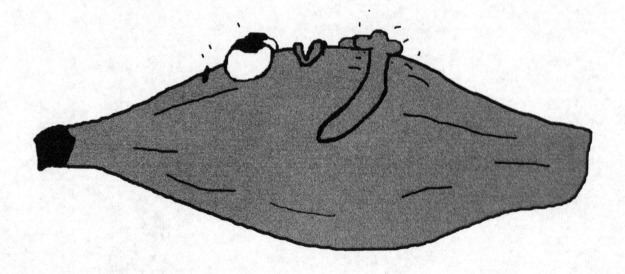

Easy Entertaining Tips

PRE-FAB IT!

For large parties, it's cheaper to make food from scratch,
but who has the time? Here are some easy short cuts
I use for most of my parties

Watermelon Basket

Dial the deli and order it!
At most stores, you'll be able to choose a style and fruit type.

Vegetable Tray

Go ahead! Pick one up!
Transfer the veggies to a lined basket or platter. Toss the tell-tale plastic containers.
Spoon the supplied dip into something or use your own dip. Be creative!
Spoon the dip into a hollowed out red cabbage or bell pepper or artichoke.
Garnish with radish flowers.

Shrimp Platter

Easy! 1 bag of frozen medium shrimp. 1 jar cocktail sauce. 2 lemons.
Thaw the shrimp by placing the frozen shrimp package in the sink.
Run cool water over it. While the shrimp is thawing, pour the sauce into a bowl.
Arrange the thawed shrimp on a platter around the cocktail sauce.
Garnish with lemons and parsley.

*If it won't be eaten right away, use a low bowl instead of a platter. Fill the bottom of the
bowl with crushed ice. Arrange the shrimp on top around the bowl of cocktail sauce.
For a snazzier sauce, add 1/2 tsp of horseradish and/or mustard.*

Salad

Get your toppings already cut up from the store.
Use packaged lettuce (rinse it 3 times and drain it on paper towels or in a salad spinner)
I like to mix store bought salads and toppings. Check out the produce and deli sections.
Serve the dressing on the side so you can use the leftovers the next day.

Visit the Deli

Pick up dishes that compliment your meal (or to be your meal)
Pastas, dips, sliced cheeses, meats, soups, toppings for salads.
It's turned into my favorite section of the store.
Well, besides the cappuccino bar.

Turn Fruit Salad into a Dessert

Serve it in wine glasses. Garnish with whipped cream or yougurt.
Top with a fresh berry and mint leaf.

Easy Shortcake

Cut angel food or pound cake into slices.
Layer with fruit and whipped cream alternating layers.
Drizzle fruit juices from fruit containers over fruit from the top.
Spoon a dollop of whipped cream on top.
Garnish with mint leaf, berry, or twisted orange.
Twisted orange...wasn't that a rock group in the 80s?

Basket of Breads

Fill a basket with different types of bite sized breads.
Smear pesto on flatbread. Top with parmesan and bake until hot.
Spread garlic, butter and parmesan on french or sour dough bread and bake.
Or buy pre-done breads from your local bakery.
Serve with little bowls of olive oil and balsamic vinegar for dipping.

Pot Luck

This is always a good one.
When friends ask what they can bring...tell them!

Charcuterie boards

Don't be afraid of them
It's just a way to keep from doing so many dishes...

Basically, you put all your hors d'oeuvres one board
or better yet, the counter (lined with foil or paper).

Design is the Key
Make it pretty, have different levels

Meat Roses

Lay salami or any type of deli meat over the rim of a glass
keep adding slices around the rim
then turn over onto the board and Voila!

Dips 'n Things

Use small dip/candy dishes, lettuce leaves/greens and fresh fruit and veggie shells
for your dip and other contents.

Decorate

With fruit and veggies and any items from your theme.
Ideas: Hot wheels or Shopkins for kids parties, pretty tea cups etc.

Cheese & Crackers

An all-time fav. Use the stick cheese and cut into slices.
Or pre-fab it with sliced cheese cut into squares.
Add your fav crackers. Alternate cheese and crackers to make a pattern.
Garnish with little bowls of spreadable cheese and sugared nuts or pretzels.
Grapes are a nice complement to cheese and crackers.
For kids parties, cut the grapes in half so they don't choke.

Themes

There are all kinds of themes for the foods on your boards.
Sweet, Savory, and The Whole Meal

Cookie Boards

Let 'em decorate cookies. Get some cookies from the store. Add frosting you can spread and frosting you can squirt to make shapes and spell names. Candy bits, marshmallows, chocolate pieces and other deliciously fun things.

Savory

Carmelize some yellow onions and bell peppers (Red, Orange and Yellow)
Stir in a can of diced green chilis.
Serve that as a garnish to a meat or plant based meat tray.
Add flatbread. You can spread pesto on flatbread or Naan and bake until the bread is slightly golden brown. Slice into little rectangles or squares.
Make a pattern by alternating your food items.
Serve hot, with a balsamic vinegar and olive oil dip.

Sandwich Boards

Bread, buns, meat, cheese, lettuce, tomato, onion, olives, mustard,
Italian dressing, Ranch dressing, pickles. mayo.
Do roll up deli burritos and slice into bite size pieces.
Serve with dipping sauces.

The Whole Meal

Lay it all out buffet style.
Garnish with fruit.
Let your guests mix 'n match
as they fill their plates.

Place colorful bell peppers in a bowl on your counter as a decoration.

LIGHT FARE DINNER PARTY

Pile on those carbs!

Step 1. SHOP

Deli Counter

3 types of pasta

Packaged Salads

Choose your fav salads and toppings

Bakery

Pick up dinner rolls and angel food cake

Produce Section

Cilantro or Italian Parsley (for garnishes)
Bell Peppers, tomatoes, avocado, cucumber, bananas and lemons
Use these for decoration. They'll look great in a bowl on your kitchen counter.
Later, you can use them in dishes or on you!

Check out the *For the Bod* section of this book.

Frozen Foods

Pick up a frozen berry mixture or your favorite frozen fruit.
I usually go for berries. The leftovers are great in smoothies!

You'll also need
Pesto
Grated Parmesan
Salad Dressing
1 jar of artichoke hearts (packed in water)

Step 2. PREPARE

Pasta

Arrange all three pastas in sections of one large bowl or platter.

Garnish with cilantro or Italian parsley. Serve a small dish of parmesan cheese on the side.

One of the pastas will undoubtedly be vegetable type. Snazz this one up with pesto, parmesan and artichoke hearts.

Microwave pesto sauce for about 30 seconds on high. Drain most of the oil and discard it. Stir the pesto into the pasta. Add the drained artichoke hearts, a dash of garlic powder and gently stir together.

Rolls

Place the rolls in a lined basket.

Salad

Rinse the salad and toppings. Drain or spin dry. Serve in a nice bowl. If you want to toss it in dressing, the salad leftovers will need to be thrown out as they will get soggy the next day. To use leftover salad the next day, serve the dressing on the side.

Dessert

Slice angel food cake into sections. Place inside a wine or parfait glass. (One for each guest).

Party preparation time: About 30 minutes

For added flare – Toss a thin slice of lemon into each water glass.

Mix the frozen fruit you chose in a bowl. Leave on the counter to thaw. When thawed, drain most but not all of the juice. Sprinkle cinnamon (2 Tbsp) and stir together. Spoon the fruit mixture over the angel food cake and drizzle a little juice on each one. Refrigerate. Just before serving, squirt with whipped cream. Garnish with berries.

Traditional Turkey Dinner
Call your grocer and order it!
Oh? You want to cook?

Turkey
Stuffing
Mashed Potatoes
Gravy
Cranberry Sauce
Green Salad
Carrot Salad
Dinner Rolls

Turkey & Stuffing
Preheat the oven to 425

1 Turkey
1 package stuffing mix
2 cups chopped celery
1 cup chopped onion
3 Tbsp poultry seasoning
1 Tbsp sage
1 cup chicken broth
1/2 cup butter

I usually make 4 times this much for a holiday dinner. My family loves stuffing... even mine!

Stuff the turkey from both ends with stuffing... OR stuff it with chunks of onion and apple. Make the stuffing in a separate casserole dish. Follow the directions on the stuffing box.

Cook at 425 for 30 minutes. Reduce the heat to 325.

Bake for about 20 minutes per pound or until turkey thermometer pops up. I usually cook mine until the legs fall off. Look! It's done!

Save the juices for gravy.

Health Tip - **Don't let the turkey sit out on the counter with the stuffing inside.** Turkey can have an unhealthful biochemical reaction to the combination of warm stuffing and meat sitting out for more than **A FEW MINUTES. It can make you very sick.**

Scoop out all the stuffing as soon as you take the turkey out of the oven. I usually combine this stuffing with stuffing I baked in a separate pan. When in doubt, don't stuff your turkey with stuffing. Store leftovers separate from meat.

Groovy (Gravy)

Turkey drippings
2 to 3 Tbsp poultry seasoning
2 Tbsp sage
1/2 tsp all purpose seasoning
Packages of Gravy mix (amounts depend on how many servings you want. I use a lot as people love gravy).
Water or chicken broth (for thinning, if necessary)

Heat the turkey drippings in a pan over medium heat.

In a cup, mix gravy mix with cold water or chicken broth. Stir together to get all the lumps out. Add mixture slowly to pan drippings, stirring constantly.

Stir in seasonings. Bring gravy to low boil then simmer until it reaches the desired consistency (a few minutes.)

For thicker gravy, add a mixture of flour and water. Do not add flour directly to gravy unless you want lumps.

Tip from Flo: Always use cold water when adding flour or corn starch for thickening.

Tip from Dish: You'd be amazed at the lumps you get when you add the flour directly to the gravy. However, don't let a few lumps ruin your gravy...turn it into stew!

Tip from Flo: Or use a strainer.

Options: Stretch your gravy by adding packaged gravy mix and more water.

Some people like a little milk in their gravy.

Mashed Potatoes

Potatoes (1 bag organic if possible)
If single potatoes, 6 to 8
1/2 cup butter
1/4 cup milk or water
Pepper
Salt (optional)

Scrub potatoes gently under water
Cut out any bad parts and discard.
Slice potatoes into chunks leaving the skin on. Throw them into a large pot and fill it with water.

Bring to a boil, then cook over medium heat for about 20 minutes.

If you put a lid on it, its sure to boil over and make a mess on your stove.

After cooking drain most but not all of the water. Add butter or margarine, salt, pepper and milk.

Whip with a mixer until smooth. Spoon into a bowl and garnish with a huge dab of butter.

Berry Sauce

Frozen blackberries
Frozen blueberries
Frozen strawberries
Frozen cherries
1 can whole cranberry sauce
1 small can crushed pineapple (drained)
3 Tbsp cinnamon

A little goes a long way - Save the leftovers. It's good to spread on toast the next morning.

See the *"What to do with leftovers"* section.

Thaw the frozen fruit. Place into a colander in the sink and drain.

If you'd like, put the colander in a bowl for the juice to drain into. You can use the juice later in a smoothie.

Place the drained fruit in a large bowl. Add the cranberry sauce and crushed pineapple. Sprinkle cinnamon on top. Mix together.

Refrigerate one hour. Serve.

Green Salad

You know the routine - Pre-Fab It! Or go Caesar - a bag of lettuce, croutons, caesar dressing. Rinse the lettuce. Toss together in a bowl and sprinkle with parmesan.

Carrot Salad

3 cups grated carrots
1 cup grated apple
1 cup raisins
1 Tbsp cinnamon

Plump the raisins by marinating them in a glass of water

Cold water - about 1 hour
Warm water - about 5 minutes

Drain. Mix the carrots, apples, raisins and cinnamon together.
Refrigerate until serving.

Delicious Ham Glaze

1/2 cup brown sugar
1/4 cup honey
1/4 cup molasses
1/4 cup ketchup
1/4 cup mustard

Bake ham at 325 for 1 1/2 hours, uncovered. Mix ingredients together well. Brush over ham one half hour before it's done cooking.

Get a pre-cooked and sliced ham. Nuke the glaze in the microwave in a loosely covered dish until hot.

Leave a hole for the air to escape so it doesn't explode. Brush the glaze over your ham and serve the rest in a side dish.

You may want to heat up your ham before guests arrive. If so, bake it uncovered with this delicious glaze.

Tip from Flo: Decorate the top of the ham with pineapple slices and marashino cherries on toothpicks. So pretty.

Chicken a la Olive
Cozy food your family will love!

1 Chicken (Cut up - Leave skin on)
2 cups brown rice
2 cans fat free chicken broth
1 cup chopped onion
1 small can whole grapes
1/2 cup raisins
1/2 cup black olives (pitted)
1/4 cup pimentos
1/2 cup sliced almonds
2 Tbsp olive oil
2 Tbsp poultry seasoning
1 Tbsp crushed garlic
1 Tbsp cinnamon
1 bay leaf
1 tsp thyme

Preheat oven to 425. In a baking dish, combine olive oil, onion and seasonings. Heat for 2 minutes, stirring occasionally. Pour chicken broth into pan and add chicken. Drain grapes, olives and pimentos and spread on top. Add raisins. Sprinkle seasonings and cover.

Reduce heat to 350 and bake for 1 1/2 hours.

Lemon Chicken

6 chicken breasts (skinless, boneless)
2 Tbsp lemon juice
1 Tbsp butter or olive oil
1 Tbsp chopped garlic
2 Tbsp chopped parsley
2 Tbsp grated parmesan cheese

Melt butter in skillet or heat oil. Add garlic and chicken. Cook over medium heat for 5 minutes on each side. Stir in lemon juice and parsley.
Sprinkle with parmesan.

1 package chicken flavored rice
(or brown rice and chicken broth)
1 1/2 cup broccoli

Rice: Follow directions on package.

If you are making from scratch, pour 1 cup brown or white rice into tall sauce pan. Add 2 cups of chicken broth.
Bring to boil. Reduce heat to low and cover. Cook for about 15 minutes or until the rice sucks up all the liquid and is soft.
Garnish with tiny pieces of green onion.

Serve together: Garnish with parsley. Serve wit a wedge of lemon.

Option: Dust chicken in flour before cooking.

Quick Mustard Chicken

I created this recipe before my last shopping day.
The family "loves" those days - "What's for dinner?"
"I'm not sure yet. We'll see what it is when it's done!"

Chicken strips or thighs (skinless, boneless)
Mustard
Lemon

Option: Eat out.

Saute chicken in pan. Squeeze the lemon and squirt the mustard over the chicken. Stir, while cooking over medium heat for about 5 minutes, or until chicken is done. You can add sliced onion or mushrooms if you'd like. Serve over rice or salad.

Crock Pot Parties & No-Mess Soups

CROCK POT PARTIES & NO MESS SOUPS

In the morning, get out your crock pot and turn it on low.

Vegetable Soup

1 bunch celery (chopped)
1 large yellow onion (chopped)
1 bunch parsley (chopped)
1 large cans tomatoes (cut up)
3 cloves garlic (cut up or smashed)
All purpose seasoning
Water (enough to fill pot)

Add the ingredients to your crockpot and cover It will be ready at dinnertime.

Variations -
String beans
barley
kidney beans
pasta
tomato sauce
corn
zucchini
beans (drain the juice or if you use uncooked beans, soak them in water the night
before, then drain before cooking)
rice
carrots
lentils
peas
your favorite vegetables
cayenne pepper for zip

Serve with hot crusty bread or rolls

Clam Chowder

2 large cans clams (drained)
1 can clam juice
4 to 6 large potatoes (diced)
1 bunch of celery (chopped)
2 onions (chopped)
2 Tbsp parsley
2 Tbsp black pepper
1 tsp garlic
Dash of hot sauce
All purpose seasoning
Water

Option - Add a little milk or cream.
Add corn (organic if possible)

Combine ingredients in a large pot.
Bring to boil, then simmer for 1 hour.

Quick tip - If your chowder is too thin, add powdered mashed potatoes until you get the desired consistency.

Serve in a bread bowl with oyster crackers.

Vegetarian Chili

4 cans vegetarian chili
1 bell pepper (chopped)
1/2 cup onion (minced)
1/2 cup green onion (diced)
1 diced zucchini
1/2 cup corn
1 bunch cilantro (chopped)
Dash of cumin
1/4 tsp chili powder
Garlic powder (4 or 5 shakes
1/2 cup salsa

Crock Pot - Cook all day on the low setting.

Pan - Bring to bubble then simmer for about 15 minutes.

Options - Top with cheese
Serve in bread bowls
Serve with nachos or quesadillas

Chicken Soup

Chicken (skinless, boneless)
Chicken giblets
2 tsp apple cider vinegar
4 cups chicken broth
2 cups chopped celery
1 onion (chopped)
1/2 cup minced parsley
6 cloves garlic (or 3 Tbsp garlic)
Dash of lemon
Water (to fill the pot)
Poultry seasoning
All purpose seasoning

Variations -
Cilantro
Rice
Noodles

Crock Pot - Add ingredients. Cook all day on the low setting.

To rush it - Throw everything in a pot and cook on the stove for about an hour.

If you want to make soup the old fashioned way - Start with a whole chicken. Boil it for 15 minutes then simmer for 1 hour.

Remove the chicken from your pot and tear the meat from the bones with a fork. Watch your fingers. It will be hot!. Stir the broth with a strainer to remove any small bones.

Place the boneless, shredded chicken back in the pot. Ad the other ingredients. Bring to boil, then simmer for another hour.

Homemade Mac & Cheese

1 box Large pasta shells
2 cups grated cheddar cheese
1/2 cup Parmesan Cheese
1/4 cup Butter
1/2 to 1 cup Milk
Dash of salt
2 Dashes of pepper

Variations -
Add more butter and more milk
Add more cheese
Add different types of cheese
Add diced green chilis

Crock Pot - Add ingredients. Cook all day on the low setting.

To rush it - Boil water and add pasta. When pasta is done, add the other ingredients.

Cook until cheese is melted stirring often. Add more milk to make it creamier.

To reheat - add milk and cook on low stirring often or nuke until hot.

Bouillabaisse

3 cups celery (finely diced)
1 onion (diced)
1 Tbsp garlic (crushed or 2 cloves)
4 cups clam juice
2 bay leaves
1/4 cup parsley (diced)
3 filets any type of white fish
(chopped in quarters)
water or beer

2 tsp lemon juice
Dash of saffron
1 cup dry white wine
2 cups chopped tomatoes
Shrimp (uncooked, de-veined, shelled)
Littleneck clams (live, cleaned)
Scallops
Mussels
Lobster tails
Seasoning (salt and pepper) to taste

Add ingredients to large pot or crock pot.
Add water or beer to rim of pot.
Cook for 2 hours on stove or 6 hours in crock pot.

Clean and rinse the shellfish and add all to the pot except the lobster and shrimp.

Cover pot and bring to a low boil. (Add the lobster and shrimp about 2 to 4 minutes before serving. Shrimp gets rubbery when overcooked)

Cook until clams open and shrimp turns pink.

Serve with sour dough bread and big mugs of broth on the side for dipping.

French Onion Soup

4 cups sliced onions
2 tsp flour
6 cups beef broth
1 cup swiss cheese (grated)
1 cup parmesan cheese (grated)
Toasted french bread

Brown the onions in butter. Add flour and cook for another minute. Stir in broth and bring to boil. Reduce heat and simmer for 15 minutes.

Pour soup into oven-safe bowls. Add 2 slices of toasted bread to each bowl. Cover with equal amounts of cheese. Broil until bubby, but not burnt. It doesn't take long. I usually keep my eyes on it so I don't forget what I'm doing.

Diane's French Onion Soup

3 large onions, thinly sliced
1/4 cup butter
3 cloves crushed garlic
Thyme to taste
4 to 5 cups water
1 large package seaweed
8 slices crusty french bread
1 cup shredded Swiss cheese

Saute onions very slowly with garlic in butter for 30 minutes. Add water and seaweed. Bring to rapid boil for 5 minutes. Lower flame, cover and simmer for at least one hour.

Place bread in bowls and ladle soup over them. Cover with cheese. Broil until cheese browns just a little.

If you want real gumbo go pick some up seafood soup

1 cup sweet corn
1 cup lima beans
2 cups stewed tomatoes (cut up)
1/2 cup chicken broth
1 cup medium shrimp (shelled and deveined)
1 cup cubed chicken breast (skinless, boneless)
1 cup okra (sliced)
1/2 cup onion (sliced)
1 cup bell pepper (chopped)
3 Tbsp diced green chilis
3 Tbsp crushed garlic
1/4 tsp allspice
1/4 tsp cayenne
1/8 tsp cumin
1/4 tsp black pepper
3 cups cooked brown rice

Add vegetables and broth into pot and bring to rapid boil. Continue to cook for 3 minutes stirring occasionally.

Add seasonings and chicken. Reduce heat to med-high and saute for 5 more minutes.

Stir in rice and shrimp. Cook until ingredients are hot and shrimp is pink.

Serve with good bread.

Spiced Cider

Apple juice
6 whole cinnamon sticks
1 tsp whole allspice
1 Tbsp whole cloves

Fill a crock pot with apple juice. Add spices. Turn crock pot on to med-low. After liquid is hot reduce heat to low. Display cups nicely next to crock pot.

Split Pea Soup

1 cup sweet corn
1 cup lima beans
2 cups stewed tomatoes (cut up)
1/2 cup chicken broth
1 cup medium shrimp (shelled and deveined)
1 cup cubed chicken breast (skinless, boneless)
1 cup okra (sliced)
1/2 cup onion (sliced)
1 cup bell pepper (chopped)
3 Tbsp diced green chilis
3 Tbsp crushed garlic
1/4 tsp allspice
1/4 tsp cayenne
1/8 tsp cumin
1/4 tsp black pepper
3 cups cooked brown rice

Add vegetables and broth into pot and bring to rapid boil. Continue to cook for 3 minutes stirring occasionally.

Add seasonings and chicken. Reduce heat to med-high and saute for 5 more minutes.

Stir in rice and shrimp. Cook until ingredients are hot and shrimp is pink.

Serve with good bread.

Tip from Dish: Take my word for it. Don't use a pressure cooker with this one - unless you really want to re-paint the kitchen. It's incredible! One tiny, little, half of a pea gets stuck in the nozzle of the pressure cooker and KABOOM! Splat! Plop, plop, plop. Months later you're still burning peas every time you make toast.

Flo: Months later?

Rabbit Food

RABBIT FOOD

Chewing is a great way to exercise!

Chinese Chicken Salad

1 small package won ton skins
4 to 6 chicken breasts (boneless, skinless)
1 to 2 heads lettuce
3 green onions
Cilantro
Slivered almonds (toasted)
Sesame seeds

Dressing:
1 Tbsp toasted sesame seeds
1/2 cup vegetable oil
2 Tbsp sesame oil
2 Tbsp sugar
1 tsp pepper
pinch of salt (optional)
4 Tbsp rice vinegar

Cut won ton skins into strips
Fry until golden brown. Drain on paper towel.

Boil chicken or cook in butter until done. Break apart lettuce. Chop green onions including most of the stem. Chop cilantro.

Combine salad ingredients, except won tons. Prepare dressing and mix well. Add dressing to salad and toss. Add won ton on top. Serve.

Pre-fab Chinese Chicken Salad

Cooked chicken from grocer
1 bunch romain lettuce
1 bunch red leaf lettuce
1 package raw cole slaw mix
2 green onions
1/8 cup Cilantro
1 package slivered almonds
1 package won tons
1 can mandarin oranges (drained)
Salad dressing (your preference)

Option: add sliced grapes
Use seared ahi/tuna instead of chicken
(tell your butcher it is for sashimi)

Wash veggies and drain on paper towel. Chop lettuces and place in a serving bowl. Add cabbage or cole slaw mix. Toss all gently.

Separate chicken meat from bones (if any) and place shredded chicken on top of lettuces.

Chop green onions and cilantro. Add to bowl. Sprinkle some mandarin orange slices on top.

Serve tossed with dressing or dressing on the side if you want to use the leftovers.

Cucumber Salad

2 cucumbers (thinly sliced)
1 red onion (thinly sliced)
1/4 cup seasoned rice vinegar

Combine ingredients in a bowl.
Cover and refrigerate for 1 hour.

Lillian's Cole Slaw

3/4 cup sugar
1 large cabbage (sliced thin or use a
couple bags of shredded cabbage)
2 large red onions (thinly sliced)

Dressing:
1 tsp celery seed
1 tsp sugar
1 tsp dry mustard
1/2 tsp salt (optional)
1 cup apple cider vinegar
1 cup safflower oil

Option: add cucumber to celery and
onion mixture. Use less oil if you'd like.

Place half of the cabbage in a large bowl and stir in sugar. Add half of the onions. Then add the rest of the cabbage and onions. Set aside.

In a saucepan combine all the ingredients EXCEPT the oil. Bring to a boil stirring occasionally. Stir in oil and bring back to boil. Pour hot dressing mix over cabbage mixture. DO NOT STIR.

Cover and chill for 24 hours. Stir before serving.

Carrot Apple Casserole

Thinly sliced carrots
Thinly sliced apples
Sugar or substitute (or nothing)
Cinnamon

The amounts depend on how many you are serving and how much you want.

Grease a baking dish. Layer carrots and apples. Sprinkle with cinnamon.
Add a couple dabs of butter.
Bake at 350 until tender.

If you use honey instead of sugar, just drizzle a little on top of the carrots and apples. You won't need much, if any.

Roasted Salad

Fresh green beans
Corn
Avocado (cut into cubes)
Tomato (chopped)
Zucchini (sliced)
Yellow squash (sliced)
Cilantro or parsley (diced)
Roasted chicken (cut up) or shrimp
Lettuce (chopped)
Olive oil
Balsamic vinegar

Option: use your fav dressing instead of the olive oil and vinegar

Saute ingredients together in tsp of olive oil and 1 tbsp of balsamic vinegar.

Cook over high heat, stirring constantly for 2 to 3 minutes. Add all purpose seasoning and 2 cups of chopped lettuce. Toss and serve.

Tip: If you have time, roast the veggies in the oven for 3 to 5 minutes at 400 degrees instead of frying. It adds a nice flavor to the vegetables!

Jack's Rizutto

Fresh spinach (washed thoroughly)
Rice (cooked)
Olives (diced)
Tomato (chopped)
Onion (chopped)
Artichoke hearts (drained)
Eggplant (cubed)
All purpose seasoning
Black Pepper

Balsamic, rice or apple cider vinegar (whichever one you like)

Option: Add a tad of olive oil or your favorite dressing.

Chop the vegetables and saute together. Add rice and cook for another 2 to 3 minutes.

Toss in a little balsamic, rice or apple cider vinegar. Sprinkle with all purpose seasoning and black pepper.

Robin's Pea Salad

30 oz defrosted peas
1 lb bacon (chopped and cooked)
1 bunch green onions
8 oz sour cream
1 Tbsp mayonnaise
Salt and pepper to taste

Mix together and refrigerate for 3 hours. Stir before serving.

Chop 'Til You Drop Salad

Use fresh veggies:
1 cup corn
1/2 cup cilantro (minced)
2 or 3 tomatoes (chopped)
1 zucchini (cubed)
6 green onions (diced)
1 red cabbage (sliced)
1 head romaine lettuce (shredded)
1 cup spinach (torn or chopped)
1/4 cup mushrooms (sliced)
1/2 cup string beans (sliced at an angle)
1/2 cup peas (or pea pods, sliced at an angle)
1/4 cup beets (grated)
1/2 cup carrots (grated)
1/2 cup broccoli (chopped)
1/2 cup red onion (minced)

Dressing ideas:
1/4 cup balsamic vinegar, 1 tsp crushed garlic, all purpose seasoning, a touch of olive oil

or

Seasoned rice vinegar and a dash of sesame oil

Place the lettuce, spinach and red cabbage in a bowl and toss. Layer the other ingredients on top. Toss just before serving. *(So your company gets to see how pretty it is!*

Spinach Mashed Potatoes

9 Potatoes (cubed)
1/2 red onion (diced)
1/2 cup green onion (chopped)
2 cups spinach (washed and drained)
2 tsp crushed garlic
3 Tbsp butter or yogurt
Parmesan cheese

Cook potatoes in a large pot of water, uncovered. Bring to rapid boil. Reduce heat and cook for about 25 minutes until potatoes are soft. Drain.

Mix in garlic, butter (or yogurt). Beat until smooth. Add onions and spinach. Stir and serve. Salt and pepper to taste. Sprinkle with parmesan.

Mom's labor of Love Salad Mix

Basic salad mix:
1 red bell pepper
3 zucchini
1/2 bunch cilantro
3 to 6 green beans
Fresh corn (cut the kernels from 3 or 4 ears of corn)

Optional ingredients to vary flavor:
Red onion
Cucumber
Tomato
Carrot
Cooked chicken
Tortilla chips

Note: The basic salad mix is fabulous in omelets!

Chop veggies into pieces about the size of your "pinkie" fingernail (*your* nail, Doll, not the enamel one). Mix together in a bowl.

Low Cal 1000 Island Salad

4 cups romaine lettuce
2 cups basic salad mix (from prior page)
1 cup cooked chicken

Dressing:
1/2 cup low-fat yogurt
1/2 cup Thousand Island dressing

Toss (only as far as the bowl).

Add chicken and decorate with a few blue corn chips.

This makes enough for several individual salads. Mix up ahead of time and store in the fridge covered. Use for several days!

Chicken Salad

4 cups romaine lettuce
2 cups basic salad mix
4 green onions (diced)
1 cup cooked chicken (cut up)

Toss together. Add bottled dressing.

Santa Fe Salad

2 cups basic salad mix
3 cups corn
1/2 cup additional chopped cilantro
1/4 cup green onions (diced)
1/4 cup red onion (chopped)
1 cup shredded chicken (cooked)
Lettuce leaves

Option: Have your mom bring it.

Mix together. Toss with a small amount of chicken.

Lay lettuce leaves on a platter. Spoon salad mixture onto lettuce leaves in a mound.

Sprinkle more shredded chicken on top. Garnish with more chopped red bell pepper, cilantro and blue corn chips.

Serve with a salad dressing of your choice.

NO KIDDING!
YOU WANT TO COOK BREAKFAST?

Vegetable Omelette

The Snow White Way - After greeting your backyard bunnies and birds, pick fresh bell pepper, green onion, broccoli, spinach and tomato from your garden. Bring them into you cottage and place them on the counter beside the dazzline bouquet of flowers you've just arranged. Wash and chop the vegetables, one by one.

Saute the colorful vegetables in a pat of butter over medium heat for about a minute or two. Place the cooked vegetables on a side plate you made on your pottery wheel until you're ready for them.

Collect 3 eggs from you beautifully coifed french hens. Beat the eggs while melting a pat of butter in the frying pan on medium heat. Pour the eggs into the pan and turn the heat to low. After the eggs start to bubble, flip gently and add the braised vegetables. Sprinkle with grated cheese. Cover the pan and cook on low until the cheese melts. Fold the omelette carefully onto a plate and garnish it with a lovely cluster of frosted red grapes freshly collected from your vines.

The Pre-Fab Way - Take the lettuce out of last night's salad and toss the leftovers (not the lettuce) in a frying pan with some eggs and cheese. Cook over medium heat, scraping the bottom of the pan with a spatula once in a while. Serve with bagels.

So it's not an omelette. You want an omelette, go to Snow White's house.

Mom's Cinnamon Rolls

It wouldn't be Christmas morning without the smell of something wonderful burning in the kitchen.

Any ready-made cinnamon rolls (with raisins if they have them)

Remove cellophane.
Wrap cinnamon rolls in foil.
Place in 425 degree oven.
Wait for the smoke alarm to go off.
Let the rolls cool, then toss in the garbage.

Tip from Flo: Keep a container of salt handy to put out those pesky fires.

Baltic Delight

Plain yogurt
Fresh fruit
Bran muffin

Tip from Dish: Save any leftover yogurt for a moisturizing facial!

Blueberry Muffins

1 package blueberry muffin mix (or any muffin mix)

Follow directions on the package
You'll probably need an egg
Water

Add in:
2 Tbsp cinnamon
1/2 cup fresh or frozen blueberries
1/2 cup walnuts (chopped)

Note: if you use frozen blueberries use a few Tbsp less liquid that the recipe on the box calls for.

Zucchini Pancakes & Waffles

For pancakes or waffles
1/2 cup grated zucchini
1 Tbsp cinnamon
1/2 tsp vanilla
eggs (# according to recipe on box)

Option: Substitute warm jelly or honey for syrup or try a fresh fruit puree on top!

Tip from Flo: Make extra and freeze them in individual servings. Very handy during the work week. Just toast them until warm and serve as usual.

Use your standard pancake of waffle mix or Bisquick and follow directions on box. Add zucchini, cinnamon and vanilla.

Separate the egg whites from the yolks. Add the yolks to the pancake or waffle mix, or leave them out entirely. Whip the egg whites until they form little peaks, then fold them gently into the mix. Do not over mix. the batter should be slightly lumpy.

Cook as described on package until golden

Zucchini Bread

3 eggs
1 cup oil
2 cups brown sugar
2 cups zucchini (grated)
2 tsp vanilla

Then add:
3 cups flour
1 tsp baking soda
1/4 tsp baking powder
3 Tbsp cinnamon
1/2 cup chopped walnuts

Option: Add raisins and/or blueberries
You can substitute apple sauce for oil to make a fat free bread. It does change the consistency. Try it a day before your event, so you can do it over if you don't like it.

Mix together

Pour into greased and floured baking pan.
Bake at 325 for 75 minutes

Todd's Scrambled Eggs

One dozen eggs
1 bell pepper (chopped)
6 green onions (diced)
1/4 cup diced green chiles
1 tomato (chopped)
6 mushrooms (sliced)
1/2 cup onion (chopped)
1 zucchini (chopped)
1/2 cup salsa
All purpose seasoning like Mrs. Dash
Last night's leftover meat (cubed)

Option: Add shredded cheese

Saute vegetables and meat in butter over medium heat. Scramble eggs and pour into pan stirring occasionally.

Top the eggs with salsa.

Roll cooked eggs in warm tortillas or serve with hot biscuits and gravy.

Cinnamon French Toast

Eggs
1 tsp vanilla
2 Tbsp cinnamon
Sliced bread
Milk

Tip from Flo: Make extra and freeze them in individual servings. Just toast and serve.

Whip mixture together. Use one egg for each slice of bread. Add a few Tbsp of milk or not more than 1/4 cup.

Drop bread in mixture and soak for 1 minute on each side.

Saute egged bread in butter for about 2 minutes on medium heat. Sprinkle with cinnamon while cooking. Turn and cook the other side until golden brown.

Serve with hot maple syrup.

Option: Sprinkle with powdered sugar. Serve with jelly and/or fresh fruit like blueberries or sliced strawberries.

Breakfast Burritos from Remod Todd

6 eggs
Refried or vegetarian beans
Diced green chilis
2 green onions (chopped)
1 tomato (diced)
Shredded cheese
Salsa
Flour tortillas

Tip from Flo: This dish tastes better when the beans are cooked the old fashioned way, on the stove (rather than microwaved)

Saute onions and tomato in butter over medium heat for about a minute. Scramble eggs and pour into pan. Add green chilis and salsa. Cook until eggs are fluffy, stirring occasionally.

Heat beans until bubbly. Spread beans on tortillas. Add cheese, scrambled eggs and salsa. Roll up.

You can nuke the whole burrito for about 25 seconds to heat up. More will make the tortilla rubbery. If you need to heat these up, place them all in a pan, cover with foil and heat in a 350 to 400 degree oven for

Fresh Hot Muffins

1 package of your favorite muffin mix
1 Tbsp cinnamon
1 cup fresh fruit or raisins
1 cup chopped walnuts

This recipe is great with raisins, diced apples and extra cinnamon in a bran muffin mix!

Also delicious is banana in a basic mix with 1/2 tsp nutmeg instead of cinnamon.

Other fruit ideas: Dried cranberries, fresh blueberries, dried or fresh chopped apricots, grated carrots or pitted cherries

Follow the directions on the packaged muffin mix.

Stir in spice, fruit and walnuts. Do not overmix. Spoon mixture into muffin or baking pan. Bake at 350 for 15 to 20 minutes until done.

Place fresh muffins in a lined basket. Serve hot!

Nana's Pumpkin Bread

1 1/2 cups sugar
1/2 tsp baking powder
1 tsp baking soda
Dash of salt (optional)
1 Tbsp cinnamon
1 Tbsp nutmeg
1 Tbsp cloves
1 1/2 cups flour
1 cup oil
1/2 cup water
1 cup pumpkin
2 eggs
1/2 cup chopped nuts
1/2 cup raisins

Do not sift dry ingredients. Mix together in order given.

Grease and flour one large bread pan or two small loaf pans, lightly. Pour mixture into pan(s) and bake at 325 for 1 1/2 hours.

When done, remove from oven and let it stand for 5 or 6 minutes. Slip a knife between the edge of the pan. Gently glide the knife around the edges, loosening the bread. Place a serving plate upside down on top of the pan. Turn the pan upside down and the bread should fall out onto the plate.

Serve with softened butter or whipped cream cheese.

Tip from Flo: Check doneness by poking a toothpick or knife into center of bread. It if comes out clean, your break is done. If a little dough sticks to it, put it back in the oven for a few more minutes. When done, let the bread rest about 10 minutes before cutting.

Tip from Dish: If the pumpkin bread doesn't come out, tap gently on the bottom of the pan. If it still doesn't come out, give it a few hard whacks until it falls onto the plate. Now, if it's still stuck, check it to make sure it's edible.

Smell it to make sure it's not too burnt. If it's okay, slice it in the pan and let your guests serve themselves!

Or turn it into a dessert! Scoop the pumpkin bread out of the pan with a large spoon. Cover it will gobs of whipped cream and refrigertate for one hour.

See! Cooking can be fun!

SMOOTHIES

Use organic produce and filtered water whenever possible.
Mix the smoothies in your blender. Leave out the frozen yogurt for less calories.

Basic Smoothie

1 large scoop protein powder (unflavored or vanilla)
1 banana
1 cup fruit
1 cup liquid
1 cup crushed ice or (1/2 cup crushed ice and 1/2 cup frozen yogurt)

Chocolate

1 large scoop chocolate flavored protein powder, nonfat frozen yogurt, water or milk, ice.

Skinny Chocolate

Plain or vanilla protein powder, ice, 1 cup water.

Berry Delight

Plain or vanilla protein powder, nonfat frozen yogurt or sorbet, frozen blueberries, frozen blackberries, banana, 1/4 cup boysenberry juice, water or milk, crushed ice.

Tropical Breeze

Plain or vanilla protein powder, nonfat frozen yogurt, ice, banana, pineapple-coconut juice (or coconut juice and 1/4 cup fresh or frozen pineapple)

Strawberry Banana

Plain or vanilla protein powder, nonfat frozen yogurt, 1/2 cup strawberries, banana, 1/2 cup water or milk, ice. If too thick add more water or milk.

Passion Peach

Plain or vanilla protein powder, nonfat frozen yogurt, frozen peaches, water or milk, ice.

Orange Freeze

Plain or vanilla protein powder, nonfat frozen yogurt, orange juice, 1 tsp whey powder, ice.

Non-Dairy

Omit the yogurt and milk from the dairy versions. Substitute with sorbet or sherbet if you'd like, or just use ice, about 1 cup juice and/or water. Still tasty, less calories.

Tropical Cocktail

Protein powder, banana, papaya, pineapple, mango, pineapple-coconut juice or water, ice.

American Flag

Plain or vanilla protein powder, strawberries, blueberries, banana, apple juice, ice.

Berryama

Plain or vanilla protein powder, blackberries, boysenberries, strawberries, raspberries, banana, boysenberry-apple juice, ice.

Optional additions:
Powdered lecithin
Whey powder
Nonfat plain yogurt
Calcium powder
Vitamin C powder
Honey
Spirulina
Powdered Greens
Fresh spinach *(really - you won't taste it if you add a little)*

Options:
Cut the juice with half water for less sugar
Apple juice makes a good base for smoothies. So does water. Try filtered water.
You can leave out the banana in any recipe.

UDDER DECADENCE
Dairy, Desserts and Devilish Dips
This section's bad!

Crab Dip

Sourdough bread round
French bread - have the bakery slice a
fresh loaf for you and seal it tight
1 cup sour cream
4 green onions (diced)
2 cups grated cheddar cheese
8 oz cream cheese
12 oz crab meat (drained)
Hot sauce
Seasoning

Mix sour cream and cream cheese, crab meat, and green onions together in a bowl. Spread on your thighs...No, just kidding. Add seasoning and hot sauce, mix.

Cut a hole in the bread round and scoop out the insides to make a bowl. Save the scooped out bread for dipping. Save the top for decoration. Spoon the crab mixture into the bread bowl and wrap in heavy foil. Bake at 350 for 1 hour.

Add a spreading knife and serve with bread and crackers.

Creamed Corn

8 oz whipping cream
8 oz half & half
1 tsp salt (optional)
6 tsp sugar (optional)
1 pinch pepper
20 oz frozen corn (partially defrosted)
2 Tbsp butter
2 Tbsp flour

Add ingredients to saucepan.
Heat to boil then simmer for 5 minutes.
Stir and serve.

Less Creamy Creamed Corn

8 oz non-fat milk
1 pinch salt (optional)
1 pinch pepper
20 oz corn (fresh, canned or frozen)
1 Tbsp butter

Heat ingredients in a sauce pan.
Stir and serve.

Option: Corn is also good cooked plain.

Nachos

Tortilla chips
Grated cheddar cheese (Lots)
Vegetarian chili (2 cans)
1/2 cup cilantro (chopped)
1 tsp garlic powder or crushed
1/2 tsp all purpose seasoning
Salsa

Place chips in a baking pan. Smother the tortilla chips with gobs of grated cheese. Microwave on high for 2 to 4 minutes until cheese melts but don't let it bubble or the cheese will get hard.

In a saucepan, combine vegetarian chili, cilantro and spices. Bring to boil, stirring constantly.

Serve wit chili dip on the side. Garnish with salsa and a touch of cilantro.

Option: Serve with guacamole.

No Guilt allowed Chili Cheese Dip

Not much in this sucker is good for you so forget about it and enjoy!

1 large package processed cheese
8 oz package cream cheese
2 cans hot chili without beans

Turn your crockpot on low.
Add ingredients, cover and cook until melted.

Serve over tortilla chips with a side of salsa.

Tip from Flo: *This stuff really disappears at parties. You'll run out early. For a large party, have another crock pot going in the kitchen to replace the empty one.*

Tip from Dish: *It may take you a day or two to get back to normal after eating this stuff. It's so good, you'll want to eat a lot! I'm not sure whether it's the gas or the bloating that gets me more the day after, but I usually hide with the window open until it goes away.*

Decadent Spinach Mashed Potatoes

9 potatoes
4 Tbsp butter
1/2 tsp garlic (optional)
3 Tbsp milk
10 oz package frozen spinach
(thawed and well-drained)
8 oz pkg cream cheese (cut up)
1/2 cup diced artichoke hearts
Salt and pepper to taste
Parmesan cheese

Cut up the potatoes (peel them if you'd like) Add them to a large pot of water (uncovered). Bring to boil then reduce heat and cook until soft. Drain.

Add cream cheese, butter and garlic. Beat potatoes until smooth. Gradually add just enough milk to make them fluffy. Mix in spinach and artichoke hearts. Salt and pepper to taste.

Spoon mixure into greased baking dish. Cover and bake for about 30 minutes at 325 until hot.

Remove from oven and sprinkle with parmesan cheese before serving.

Beef or Turkey Burger Enchiladas

1 lb ground meat
1 onion (chopped)
Diced olives
Grated cheddar cheese
Enchilada sauce
Tortillas

Cook meat and onions together in 1tsp oil or butter.

Heat sauce. Add water if necessary. Warm tortilla in sauce then lay it in a baking dish. Add 1 Tbsp cooked meat, olives, and 2 Tbsp cheese to tortilla and roll up. Repeat. Top with more enchilada sauce. Sprinkle with more cheese.

Garnish with diced tomatoes, cilantro and salsa!

Bake at 350 for 20 to 30 minutes, or nuke on high for 4 to 5 minutes.

Stella's Carrot Cake

2 cups flour
2 cups sugar
1/4 tsp baking powder
1 tsp baking soda
1 tsp nutmeg
1 tsp cloves
1 Tbsp cinnamon
4 eggs (beaten)
1 1/2 cups vegetable oil
2 cups grated carrots
1 cup chopped walnuts

Sift the dry ingredients together. Set aside. Blend eggs and oil and mix until creamy. Add carrots to egg mixture and stir in. Add dry ingredients and blend thoroughly without stirring too much.

Pour mixture into greased and floured cake pan. Bake at 350 for 1 hour.

Icing:

8 oz package cream cheese (softened)
1/2 cup butter
1 tsp vanilla
1 lb package powdered sugar

Cream together the cream cheese and butter. Add vanilla and powdered sugar. Beat until smooth. Spread on cold cake. Garnish with chopped walnuts.

Tip from Dish: Keep your hair away from the mixing bowl.

The Very Best Rum Cake Ever!

Before you start, sample the rum to make sure it is of the finest quality. Good, isn't it? Now go ahead. Select a mixing bowl, measuring cup, etc. Now check the rum again...it must be of the highest quality. The best way to check it is to pour one level cup of rum into a glass and drink it as fast as you can. Repeat.

With an electric mixer, beat 1 cup butter in a large fluffy bowl. Add one teaspoon of thugar and beat again. Meanwhile make sure the rum is of excellent quality...try another cup. Open 2nd quart of rum if necessary. Add 2 arge leggs, 2 cups of fried druit and beat till high. If druit gets stuck in the beaters, just eject them and bang them on the counter until the druit flies out. Sample the rum again checking for tonacistity.

Nex, sift 3 cups of pepper or salt...it doesn't matter which. Test the rum again and sift 1/2 pint of jemon luice. Fold in chopped butter and whipped nuts. Add some brown thugar or whatever color you can find.

Grease oven and turn cake pan to 350 gredees. Now pour the whole mess in the oven, check the rum again and bo to ged!

1 or 2 quarts of fine rum
1 cup butter
1 tsp sugar
1 very large eggs
1 cup dried up fruit
1 tsp soda
Some baking powder
Lemon juice
Brown sugar
Nuts

Lemon Frosted Crescent Rolls

1 or 2 packages crescent dough

Filling:
8 oz cream cheese
1/4 cup sugar
1 1/2 tsp vanilla

Mix filling ingredients together. Spread on dough and roll up. Shape into crescents. Bake as per the instructions on the crescent roll package.

Frosting:
2 cups powdered sugar
1/3 cup lemon juice

Mix together. Spread over hot, fresh from the oven crescent rolls. Serve.

Pesto Crescent Rolls

1 or 2 packages crescent dough
1 or 2 packages pesto

Spread pesto generously on dough and roll up. Shape into crescents. Bake as per the instructions on the crescent roll package.

You can use any type of bread for this one. Bake at 350 until hot.

Wow! These Are Sooo Good! Bars

That's what everybody says the first time they bite into these.

1/2 cup butter or margarine
1 1/2 cup crushed graham cracker
14 oz can sweetened condensed milk
6 oz package semi-sweet chocolate chips
3 1/2 oz flaked coconut
1 cup chopped nuts

Preheat oven to 350. In a 13" x 9" pan, melt the butter. Sprinkle graham cracker over melted butter. Pour milk evenly in pan.

In a separate bowl, mix coconut, chips and nuts. Spread mixture inside pan and pat down.

Bake at 350 for 20 to 35 minutes. Cool completely. Inhale. Cut leftovers into squares. Usually makes 24 bars.

Cheesecake

Who has time to make cheesecake? Buy one from the grocery store. If it's not pretty or delish enough, add toppings:

Shaved chocolate & whipped cream - Squirt a whipped cream design on your cheesecake. Use a cheese grater to "shave" a chocolate bar into curls, then sprinkle them on the cheesecake.

Note: If you use canned whipped cream, do it immediately before serving because it will "melt". If you want the whipped cream to last longer, either use a ready made type like *cool whip* or use real whipping cream. For real whipping cream, beat it until it is stiff enough to form little peaks. Add powdered sugar if you want it to last longer.

Flavored whipped cream: Add a Tbsp of your favorite flavoring while mixing the whipped cream. (Chocolate, Hazelnut, Almond, Mocha, Rum, Kahlua, Baileys, Peppermint)

Strawberry - Mix strawberries with 2 Tbsp honey. Spoon onto cheesecake.

Blueberry - Fresh or frozen blueberries with 2 Tbsp honey.

Cherry - Canned cherry pie filling. Garnish with whipped cream.

Mix it up - Fresh raspberries, blueberries and blackberries or kiwi, banana and pineapple.

Lemon Whippersnappers

Oh my goodness!

1 package lemon cake mix
2 cups whipped topping
1 egg

Powdered sugar after baking

Mix ingredients together. Spoon dollops 1 1/2" apart on greased cookie sheet.

Bake at 350 for about 10 minutes or until golden. Drop hot cookies gently into powdered sugar. Cool.

Fudge Brownie Sundaes

Brownies (buy them from store)

Ice cream or frozen yogurt
Hot fudge topping
Whipped cream
Chopped nuts

Option - Use mint chip ice cream!

Heat fudge topping in microwave for 30 to 60 seconds.

Crumble the brownies. (I got this idea one evening after dropping the pan on the floor).

Layer parfait glasses with crumbled brownie, hot fudge and ice cream. Top with whipped cream and nuts.

Susie's Sort of Easy Almond Roca
A favorite!

1 cup butter (room temperature)
1 cup sugar
3 1/2 oz blanched slivered almonds
1 large chocolate bar
1 cup minced pecans or walnuts

Start with a cold frying pan or electric skillet and wooden spoon. Place butter and sugar in pan and cook on high heat, stirring constantly, until mixture bubbles for 10 seconds.

Add the almonds and reduce heat to 320 (or medium low) until mixture bubbles again. Stir constantly - sugar burns easily.

Increase heat to high again and stir, cooking until mixture turns a coffee with cream color.

Remove from heat and quickly pour into an ungreased 13" x 9" pan. Spread evenly.

Break up chocolate bar and place on top. As it melts, spread it evenly. Sprinkle nuts on top and press into chocolate. Cool completely, then break into pieces.

Tip from Flo: You'll have to work very fast. Have everything ready and measured before you begin. Have your ungreased 13" x 9" pan near you.

Be very careful! This hot mixture can cause severe burns!
Keep the kids and pets out of the kitchen while you are making it.

Phefferneuse

I bake these once a year - holiday season. No matter how much I make, I always run out.

2 cups flour
1 cup butter
6 Tbsp granulated sugar
1 cup walnuts
1/2 tsp vanilla
1 package powdered sugar

Sift the flour into a bowl. Add butter and granulated sugar. Cut the butter into the flour using two knives.

Then, mix the ingredients together using your (clean) hands. Batter will be "grainy" (tiny clumps of flour and butter).

Now - ***depending on the type of day you've had*** - chop the nuts into fine pieces, or **SMASH** the bag with a mallet as hard as you can, then spoon the mush into your bowl.

Roll the dough into 1/2 inch balls and place on an ungreased cookie sheet.

Tip - save your nails. Have the kids roll them into little balls. If you don't have kids, borrow some.

Bake at 350 for about 10 minutes or until golden.

Remove from oven. Using a spatula, gently place hot cookies in a bowl of powdered sugar. Roll each cookie lightly in powdered sugar.

Watch them! They'll disappear before your eyes!

Pound!
Kerplop!
Whack!

Whack! WHACK!
WHACK! WHACK!
WHACK! KERPOW!!!
WHACK! WHACK!
WHACK!!

Well, I don't have to ask how your day was.

Grace's Almond Sugar Cookies

1 cup butter
1 cup sugar
1 cup powdered sugar

Cream together until fluffy.

Add:
1 cup oil
2 eggs

Blend with sugar mixture until creamy.

Sift into fluffy, creamy mixture:
4 1/2 cups flour
1 tsp cream of tartar
1 tsp baking soda
1 1/2 tsp almond extract

Stir gently with fork until dry ingredients are mixed in. Do not overmix.

Chill for 1 hour. Roll into balls and press with fork. Bake at 350 for 10 to 12 minutes. Remove from oven and dip in sugar. Yummy.

Nana's Apple Crisp

6 apples
1/2 cup sugar

Slice apples and lay in greased baking dish. Sprinkle sugar on top.

Topping:
1/2 cup melted butter
1/2 cup brown sugar
3/4 cup flour
1/2 cup raisins

Mix together brown sugar, butter, raisins and flour. Sprinkle on top of apples. Bake at 325 for 30 minutes.

Serve hot over vanilla ice cream.

Option: **Add 1 Tbsp cinnamon**

Jewel Cookies

1 cup butter
1/4 cup brown sugar
1 egg yolk
1 tsp vanilla
1 cup flour

Topping:
1 egg white
1 cup diced walnuts or pecans
Strawberry jelly

Option: Use festive colors of jelly for different holidays and occasions!

Mix together with a fork. (For a flakier cookie, do not overmix). Refrigerate 1 hour.

Remove cookie dough from fridge and roll into 1" balls. Dip each one in egg yolk then roll in diced nuts.

Place cookie balls on lightly greased cookie sheet. Press a dent in the center of each cookie with your finger.

Bake at 375 for about 8 minutes, until done. Spoon a dollop of jelly into each cookie hole and arrange on a plate.

Aunt Dot's Peanut Butter Cookies

1 cup peanut butter
1/2 cup butter
1/2 cup sugar
1/2 cup brown sugar
1 tsp vanilla
1 egg
1 1/2 cups flour (sifted)
3/4 tsp baking soda
1/2 tsp baking powder
Dash of salt

Cream peanut butter and butter. Add sugars. Add vanilla and egg. Beat well.

Sift dry ingredients together and add to creamed mixture. Stir. Add chocolate chips or chopped nuts, if desired.

Form into little round balls. Dip fork in water then press top of each cookie ball forming a plaid pattern. Bake at 375 for 8 to 10 minutes until golden brown.

Mom's Lemon Cake

1 package lemon cake mix
1 package instant vanilla or lemon pudding
4 eggs
3/4 cup oil
1/2 cup lemon juice

Beat for five minutes on medium speed (you'll need a mixer for this one). Pour into sprayed and floured cake or molding pan. Bake at 350 for 35 to 45 minutes.

Frosting:
1 package powdered sugar
1/2 cup butter
1 tsp vanilla
1/4 cup grated lemon rind
Juice from one lemon

Beat together on medium speed until blended. Spread on cooled cake.

Mom's Party Cake

1 package yellow cake mix
1 package instant vanilla pudding
4 eggs
3/4 cup oil
3/4 cup dry sherry
1 tsp nutmeg

Beat for five minutes on medium speed. Pour into greased and floured 10 inch tube pan or bundt cake pan.

Bake at 350 for 45 minutes. Serve without frosting.

Dish's Lemon Cake

Dial the bakery. Order it! Extra lemon.

Devilish Double Rich Chocolate Cake

1 package chocolate cake mix
Egg (see package for quantity)
Oil (see package for amount)
Water (see package for amount)
1 small package chocolate chips
2 or 3 Tbsp sour cream

Follow directions on package but reduce water by 2 or 3 Tbsp. Add in sour cream and beat as directed on box. Stir in chocolate chips. Bake as directed on package.

Frosting:
1 package powdered sugar
1/2 cup butter
1 tsp vanilla
1/4 cup sour cream
Milk
Chocolate powder

Beat together until creamy.
Add chocolate powder to taste.
Add milk until it reaches desired consistency. Spread on cooled cake.

Easy Bite-Size Desserts

1 package frozen puff pastry sheets (thawed)

On a lightly floured surface, cut puff pastry dough into squares. Add about 2 Tbsp filling in the center of each square.

Filling options:
Chocolate chips
Mincemeat
Canned pie filling
cream cheese and fruit
marzipan or almond paste

Lift the corners of the square and twist together.

Place on an ungreased cookie sheet and bake at 400 for about 10 minutes until the shells are golden brown. Sprinkle with powdered sugar if desired.

Option: Mix powdered sugar and milk or lemon juice and drizzle it right after taking these from the oven so it melts onto the dessert.

Hot Cocoa

Instant cocoa mix
Water or milk
Whipped cream
Dash of cinnamon or cocoa

Pour instant cocoa into cup. Boil water or milk. If you use milk, stir constantly. Add hot liquid to the cup and stir in. Add whipped cream and topping.

or

Marshmallows
Instant cocoa mix
Water or milk

Fill a up half way with marshmallows. Pour instant cocoa into cup. Add hot liquid. Stir.

Serve with big cookies, fuzzy slippers and a fun board or card game.

Easy Cobbler

2 cans pie filling
1 yellow cake mix
2 eggs
1/3 cup water
1/4 cup melted butter

Grease a baking dish. Dump in pie filling. Mix cake mix, eggs, and water together. Spoon over fruit filling.

Drizzle melted butter and topping.

Bake at 350 for 45 minutes. Serve warm.

Topping options:
Cinnamon and Sugar - for apple filling
Coconut and nuts - for cherry filling
Flour, hard butter, cinnamon, brown
sugar - for French apple topping.

Option: Substitute frozen pie crust for cake mix. Thaw crust. Cut into strips. arrange on top of pie filling. Add butter and topping. Bake.

Puzzle Cake

**4 prepared loaf pan size cakes
(any type will do)
Whipped topping
Powdered sugar**

Tip: Use real whipping cream for this.
Beat on high until you can form little
peaks in the whipped cream.

*We got this recipe from an accident in the
kitchen. Two cake layers crumbled out of
their pans and fell on the counter. With
dinner in 5 minutes, we had to work fast.
"Glueing" the cake together with whipped
cream (and powdered sugar for stiffness),
we made an igloo. Our families thought it
was very creative...Hah! They were lucky
the cake didn't fall on the floor!*

Slice your cake into chunks or layers.
Mix 1/2 cup powdered sugar into the
whipped topping. Spread topping on layers.
Repeat until you have your desired shape.
Smooth the rest of the topping on the cake
and make little swirls with the back of a
spoon.

Cappuccino Brownies

**Packaged brownie mix (without nuts)
Read the package for the ingredients and
oven setting.**

You'll also need:
**3 Tbsp instant coffee
1 extra egg
1/4 cup flour**

Snazzy Topping:
**8 oz package cream cheese
1/3 cup sugar
1 egg
2 Tbsp flour
1 1/2 tsp cinnamon**

Mix eggs, coffee and water together before
adding them to the mix. Add egg mixture
to packaged mix and stir in other items the
brownie package calls for. Only mix enough
to blend ingredients. Mixing too much
makes the brownies tough. Spread into
greased pan.

Mix topping together. Spoon over brownie
batter and swirl wit a knife. Bake for 40
minutes. You can test if the brownies are
done by inserting a clean tableknife into the
center of the pan. If it pulls out clean (free
of gooey brownie) it is done. If not, bake it
a little longer.

Cool completely. Cut into squares. Try to
save some for your family and guests.

Culinary Delight

1 phone or computer
1 pair fuzzy slippers
1 beverage

Leisurely flip through food related sites and recipes, saving coupons as you go.

Later, take a pleasant drive toward the market. Pass by, you can shop later. Head to your favorite restaurant, or try a new one that looks cute. Order a fabulous meal. Eat!

On your way home, stop by the market. Now browse through culinary heaven relaxed with a full tummy and a wonderful sense of well being. Take an exciting walk through the deli and bakery aisles and remind yourself how much time you'll save cooking the Pre-Fab way!

Pick up packaged foods, read labels and plan your dining experiences for the week.

Take a few minutes to visit the coffee bar. (This is Flo's favorite). Organize your coupons for a speedy check out.

Then drive home, unpack your groceries and relax by the fire with a huge cup of tea and one of those saucy novels or binge watch something interesting.

Easier Cobbler

2 cans pie filling
1 pre-made frozen pie crust

Thaw pie crust. Pour pie filling into greased baking dish. Break or slice pie crust into whatever shapes you desire and lay on top of pie filling.

Bake until the pie crust pieces turn light brown.

Serve with ice cream or yogurt!

Becky's Lace Cookies

1 cup butter (softened)
1 cup brown sugar
1 cup sugar

Beat until smooth.

Then add:
1 egg
1 tsp vanilla
1 tsp baking soda
1 tsp baking powder
1 tsp salt (optional)
1 cup flour

Mix together.

Then add:
1 cup coconut
2 cups old fashioned oatmeal
1 cup semi-sweet chocolate chips

Mix together and spoon onto cookie sheet.

Bake at 350 for 8 to 10 minutes until golden brown. Do not burn.

Cool slightly then, place cookies on cooling rack or plate.

Kitchen Secrets

KITCHEN SECRETS

Make your home smell like you cooked all day while you unpack dinner and hide the containers before company arrives.

Apple Pie Smell

1 apple
2 Tbsp cinnamon
1/4 cup water

Set oven to 350. Slice one apple into quarters, place in pie pan. Add water and cinnamon. Bake until company comes. Turn off oven before it burns.

Not enough time?

Add same ingredients to saucepan. Blaze that sucker on high until it boils. Reduce heat to simmer. Take off stove and hide the pan before your guests arrive.

Garlic & Onions

The aroma of garlic and onions always makes people think something wonderful is cooking. The fastest way to do it is in a frying pan.

3 cloves garlic
(or 3 Tbsp crushed garlic from the jar)
1 onion (sliced in chunks)
3 Tbsp butter or oil (since you're not going to eat it, pile on the fat)

Cook uncovered over medium heat for 5 minutes. If you need to cook it longer to extend the smell, use low heat.

Option: Toss in some chicken. Sprinkle with poultry seasoning and squeeze a lemon over it. Simmer for 30 minutes. This one you can eat!

Air Freshener

Great for getting rid of fish odors! Place a lemon in the oven and bake for 15 minutes at 350 with the oven door open. (If you're in a rush turn it on high, but watch it. The smell of burnt lemon isn't much better than old fish.)

HOW TO GET RID OF UNWANTED GUESTS

Surprise! Surprise! You have company! You had other plans, but now you have company. Don't sweat it, Doll. Here are some ways to get rid of them without having to be rude.

Ahh - The Smell Of It

Offer them coffee and go into the kitchen. Get out a large pot and fill it with about 4 inches of water. Chop a cabbage into quarters and toss in the pot. Add 1 cup vinegar. Bring to a boil uncovered. Sit down and chat for a moment. The aroma of boiling cabbage is quite an unusual one. Wait until its pungence permeates the room, then invite your friends to dinner. You'd better get their coats. They'll be running for the door.

What's That On Your Leg?

Ask your surprise guests to come in, but tell them to watch their step. Tell them your son just spilled his flea circus on the carpet. Get out the vacuum cleaner and say, "How nice of you to stop by!" If they're still there when you finish vacuuming, ask them, "You're not allergic to bug spay are you?...Or flea bites?" Your guests should be leaving now. If they don't try the next suggestion.

The Tired Act

Invite your friends to have a seat and ask them how they've been. As they tell you, start to nod off. Don't snore though, you'll start laughing and give it away. Pretend you're really tired and you are trying to keep your eyes open. Let your head sink suddenly then jerk it back up. Open your eyes REALLY WIDE and ask another question. Blink a lot. They'll either get the hint or think your hairdo's too heavy.

Getting Really Dense People to Leave

Use this only as a last resort. Stick out your chin, force a smile so wide it makes the skin bunch up around your ears, bug your eyes out really big and growl at them without letting them answer back, "How are you? I'm fine. I always look this way this time of the month. PMS. Do you have chocolate? Leave now if you want to live. Run! Run!" You probably wont' hear from them in awhile. If you see men in white coats walking up your driveway, hide and lock the door.

Last Resort

Truth.
"Dude, come on, I'll walk you out and see ya another time."

New ideas may flow in from unexpected places.
Some may even be good.

FLO'S CORNER
Creative ways to slice and dice

How to make vegetable flowers

You can use radishes, celery, green onions, and carrots to make garnishes.

Take a 2 to 3 inch long piece of vegetable or a radish.
Cut a checkerboard pattern in one end, lengthwise, about 1/3 of the length.

Place the cut vegetables in a bowl of ice water for about 10 minutes.
Then use as to decorate your dishes.

You can make another "flower" by cutting 5 or 6 thin V-shaped grooves in a vegetable.

After grooves are made, slice the vegetable into thin slices.

In most cases, you will have something that resembles a flower.
Radishes, carrots, cucumber, yellow squash, zucchini, mushrooms,
and eggplant work well for this version.

On larger "flowers" you can use a small round cookie cutter to cut out centers.
Mix and match your "flowers" and centers.
(Carrot center on cucumber flower, etc.
You can also use fruit.

Leaves

Long, thin green onions, bok choy, dandelion or cilantro pieces make fabulous leaves.

Curls

Use a peeler to cut long, thin strips. They should naturally curl up.
Chill in ice water until you are ready to serve.

Shapes

You can use cookie cutters to make shapes from sliced fruit and vegetables.
If the fruit is small, make a slice and stick sections together like a Picasso painting.

Dip Bowls

Create your own bowls for cold party dip.
Good veggies for bowls are tight red or green cabbage, bell peppers, jicama, tomatoes.
Place them on a platter lined with lettuce leaves.

Cabbage - Use the core as the bottom. Slice a little off the top then use a bent grapefruit knife to cut out the bowl. If you don't have a grapefruit knife, just do your best to cut a little bowl in the cabbage. (Don't go too deep.) Fill your bowl with dip.

Jicama - Same as cabbage. This is a little more difficult to make.

Bell Pepper - Choose peppers with even bottom and wide round shapes. Pick a pepper that will stand up. Cut out the core and clean out the seeds. Rinse, dry and fill with dip.

Tomato - Tomatoes are great as individual dip bowls. With the stem at the top, cut the top off and scoop a bowl shape in the tomato. Fill with dip or tuna salad.

Artichokes - Cook artichokes in water until tender (about 1 hour). Carefully remove the center leaves making sure to leave the base and surrounding leaves intact. Arrange the leaves around the artichoke on an attractive platter.

Lemon Twists

Slice a lemon into thin wheels. You can use them as is, or cut them in half and twist. If you'd like, you can use the peels to snazz up water glasses. Cut the lemon peel into 1/4" wide, 1 1/2 inch long strips. Twist them over the water glass to release the flavor, then drop in.

Pear Bunnies

Great fun at spring and birthday parties!

Pear halves
Red grapes
Raisins
Carrots
Cottage cheese or yogurt
Orange slices
Whipped cream

Use a pear half for the bunny body. Cut the grape in half and use for eyes. Use the raisins as a nose. Slice the carrots diagonally into 1 inch slivers, and use them for ears. Lay a lettuce leaf on a plate. Add a mound of cottage cheese or yogurt. Place the bunny on the mound. Squirt a tad of whipped cream for the tail. Garnish with orange slices.

Orange Boats

Cut an orange in half. Scoop out the insides and fill it up with chopped fruit. Cut a thin slice from the other half of the orange and stick a toothpick through it. Stick the toothpick in the center of the orange boat to make a sail. Cut a tiny thin piece of lemon and poke a toothpick through it. Stick the toothpick through the top of the "orange-sail" to make a flag Serve on a lettuce leaf and garnish with a sprig of mint.

Fruit Bowls

Many types of fruit make marvelous bowls. Melons, apples, orange, or any other round shaped fruit will do nicely. Cut an alternating V shaped pattern in the middle of the fruit. Go all the way around until it comes apart. Scoop the insides out and fill with yogurt or fresh fruit. Go crazy and cut your fruit bowl into a basket shape! Or - Make your fruit resemble a fish or car by cutting accents into the sides and adding "fins" or "wheels." Garnish with those cute little umbrellas or plastic pink flamingos.

COOKING WITH HERBS

Herbs are best when fresh, if possible.

Basil -
There are many types of fresh basil. The green, standard leaf basil that you get from the grocery store is the sweetest. Use it in Italian cuisine. Basil flowers are edible, pretty and quite spicy. Pick off the flower pods and sprinkle on your favorite pasta! Tip for easy basil strips - Pull leaves off and stack them. Roll the leaves up into a tube shape, then cut. If you grow basil in your garden, pick stems before they flower.

Opal Basil -
A beautiful, purple basil that is a bit stonger and spicier than the green basil. Add it to bottled apple cider vinegar for use on salads and other dishes.

Chives -
They have the cutest little purple flowers in the spring! Chives add a bit of zing to baked potatoes, omelets and salads. You can also eat the flowers. Cut them up and use sparingly, as they have a stronger flavor than the leaves.

Dill -
Fabulous on fish! Dice and add tomato to archichoke dip!

Garlic -
We love garlic! It's wonderful in many dishes and fabulous in the garden. I grow it near my roses to keep the aphids away. It has also been said to keep away colds. (That's because people don't come near you after you eat a lot of it.)

Oregano -
The familiar herb in Italian sauces, oregano has a hearty, robust flavor. It's great on meats and in soups, too.

Mint -
Delicious in iced tea! Nice garnish too. If you grow it, plant it in a pot. If you put it in your garden it will take over like a weed.

Poultry seasoning - Use in chicken dishes. Just like Mom used to make before she taught you how to cook!

Rosemary -
Wonderful in bottled vinegars. Fabulous on lamb or chicken. Remove the leaves and save the stems. You can use the leaves in cooking and use the wood-like stems as skewers for kabobs!

Sage -

Used quite often in holiday meals. Sage has a slightly bitter, musty taste. Use it in poultry and stuffing.

Thyme -

Thyme is good on almost anything. It adds a light, minty, almost lemony flavor to fish, chicken and vegetables.

Tarragon -

Often used in bouquet garni, tarragon has a light, licorice taste. Flavor sauces, meats, vinegar and fish with tarragon.

FRESH HERB OIL & VINEGARS
They make wonderful gifts!

Flavored Oil

1 quart jar bottle and cork
Olive oil
1 large rosemary sprig
2 to 3 cloves garlic
2 red or orange bell peppers
Garlic flowers

Put the cork inside the bottle. Notice where the bottom of the cork is. You will want to only fill your bottle to just below that point.

Remove cork and insert herbs, flowers and vegetables into bottle.

Make a homemade tag by cutting paper into a rectangle or other shape. Fold in half and punch a hole in one corner. Write contents on the front of the tag and to/from info on the inside. Poke a ribbon through the hole and tie around the neck of the bottle.

Flavored Vinegar

1 quart jar bottle and cork
10 thin chives
Small basil sprigs
Rice vinegar
Raffia bow

Options:
Baby carrots
Red chili peppers
Mixed colored peppercorns
Basil
Italian parsley
Dill
Garlic cloves
Balsamic vinegar
Apple cider vinegar
Edible flowers

After you make make your flavored vinega, put the cork firmly inside the bottle.

Make a homemade tag and attach with a ribbon.

It's also fun to use a wax stamp set to stamp your own insignia on the bottle. Place a few pretty herbs or flowers and a ribbon on the face of the bottle. Pour enough wax on them to attach them to the bottle, then seal it with your stamp.

You can decorate the bottles with buttons and bows, or artificial flowers, gems, stones. Use a hot glue gun and your imagination!

TIPS

How to get that garlic smell off your fingers

Place your fingers on a stainless steel kitchen knife or spoon and run it under cold water for about 10 seconds. The reaction between the stainless steel and the water removes the odor.

Salt substitute

A slice of lemon squeezed over cooked chicken adds a nice, tangy flavor.
It's also good over steamed veggies.

Buy fresh berries in the summer

They're cheaper when they are in season. Wash, clean, double wrap and freeze them to use later in the year. Also try making berry puree. Freeze in small containers to use like syrup.

Oil substitute

Use apple sauce instead of oil to bake desserts the low-fat way.
It's good in most quick breads, brownies and cakes.
Not as moist as oil though.

Ripening avocados

Toss the avocados in a paper bag and lay them in a shady spot overnight.
Really green avocados may take longer.
(Note: Placing them in the sun will turn them brown. Don't ask me how I know.)

Keep fruit salad from turning brown

Squeeze a little juice from lemon, lime, orange or pineapple over the fruit.
Note: If you use too much it will change the taste of the fruit.

Fresh celery and carrot sticks

Stay fresher longer in a container of cold water, in the fridge.
I keep my nail polish in the fridge too! Not packed in water though.

Chop onions without tears

Store your onions in the refrigerator. Rinse them in cold water before cutting.

Storing different types of fruit

Some types of fruit release gases which can cause others to ripen and spoil faster than usual. Store citrus separate from other types of fruit. Potatoes should not be stored near apples. Bananas are best stored by themselves since they bruise easily.

Try wrapping plastic wrap around the stems of the bunch of bananas.
They say it's supposed to extend the life of the bananas a little.

Carpet and room fresheners

Baking soda is a great carpet freshener.
Sprinkle it on the carpet. Wait 5 minutes then vacuum up.

Vinegar relief

Always keep some vinegar in the house. It's great for:

Getting out stains - Mix 1 part vinegar to 3 parts water. Dab into stain.
Blot with a dry towel. Works well on pet stains if you get them early enough.

Getting odors off hands - Pour a little vinegar over your hands, then wash thoroughly.

Helping to protect against bacteria - 1 part apple cider vinegar to 6 parts water. Drink it.
It helps cleanse the system. Rinse your mouth out with plain water afterwards.

Helping to prevent salmonella poisoning - Rinse your chicken in half vinegar
and half water mixture. Let it sit for a minute or two in another dish.
(Never re-use the same dish or package the chicken came in).
Rinse with plain water. Cook normally.

Lemon degreaser

To remove grease and food odors from your hands, squeeze fresh lemon over them
then was your hands normally.

Fresh Drains

Pour baking soda in sink and tub drains to freshen them up.
Let sit a couple of hours or overnight before rinsing.

A Clean Kitchen is a Healthy Kitchen

These days, we need to protect ourselves from harmful bacteria in our food.
Here are some tips:

Wash utensils thoroughly - I wash my knives and spoons
between each thing I'm making or chopping.

Keep your cutting board clean - They say plastic cutting boards are best, but I use a wood one more often. I clean it in between each thing I am chopping. I don't use it for meat though. If I did, I would wash it thoroughly and perhaps pour vinegar over it to clean it thoroughly from hiding bacteria. After cleaning the cutting board dry it thoroughly. Even when cutting veggies, I wash the cutting board between each variety.
Yes, it may be overdoing it a bit, but I haven't gotten sick in...
well, you don't really care how old I am, do you?

Hydrogen Peroxide

Keep it handy in the kitchen and bathroom

Great kitchen disinfectant!
Use a cleaning solution of 1 part hydrogen peroxide to 6 parts water.
Use it to disinfect cutting boards, counter tops, dishwasher, etc. If you use it on surfaces you cut food on, or eat on, rinse them off with water after, just to remove any chemical taste.

Clean your toothbrush
Pour hydrogen peroxide on your toothbrush or dip the toothbrush into a small container filled with hydrogen peroxide. It will bubble up.
Let that happen for a few minutes then rinse in hot water.

Smoking Ovens

Pour salt or baking soda over messy oven spills to help stop the smoke.
It also breaks down the burnt stuff to make cleaning up easier.
When the oven is cool, scrape the spill off with a spatula.

Disposal

After squeezing lemons on your favorite dishes, toss the lemon into the disposal and run with water. The lemon rind helps to remove grime and leaves a nice scent. You can pour your old boxes of baking soda down the drain to freshen it up, too.

Kitchen Fires

Salt is a great kitchen helper! Throw it on a fire in a frying pan and put the lid on it.
Use it to put oven fires out, and reduce smoking from burnt food that
dripped onto the bottom of the oven.

Baking soda works too. In fact, if you have an electric stove,
baking soda seems to work better on a stove fire.

NEVER throw WATER on a grease fire. It spreads the flames and could splatter on you.

It's a good idea to keep a fire extinguisher near the kitchen, too.
Note: Be sure to get the correct type for a grease fire.
Also, check the expiration date on your fire extinguisher once a year. Check online
to see if there is a local place you can refresh your fire extinguisher's content.

Keep your hair away from the flames.
Hair spray, nail polish and some types of makeup are flammable. So are scrunchies.

Use Ice for Discomfort

A little ice water can help wash excess stomach acid from the esophagus, thus relieving
the burning sensation in your throat. Don't drink too much though, or it could hamper
digestion. Ice is also a great relief for muscle strains and bruises, headaches and neck pain.
A bag of frozen peas isn't bad either. Neither is a cocktail.

Headaches

Avoid bananas, walnuts, chocolate, sweets and caffeine if possible, if you suffer from
headaches often. These may have contributed to your headache in the first place and may
intensify the pain. Try some fresh fruit (not bananas) and drink lots of water.
Some say that drinking regular iced tea (not coffee) can help relieve the pain from
a headache. A massage is nice too.

There is a pressure point at the top of both forearms (just below the elbow) that is very
sensitive. If you feel around on your arm and find a point that hurts when you press on it,
you've probably found it. Pressing gently on these acupressure points for about 16 seconds
at a time may relieve pain from your headache. At the very least, it will divert
your attention from the pain in your head to the new pain in your arms.

When nothing else works, you might turn off all the lights and noise, then lie down and
close your eyes with a cold compress over your eyes and forehead. Relax and take a nap.
The world will wait for you. If your headache persists, you might see a doctor.

Food Combining for Better Digestion

Eating certain foods together can make it easier,
or more difficult on your digestive tract.

Vegetables with carbohydrates (pasta, rice, potatoes, etc) is good
Meat with vegetables is good
Fruit is best eaten by itself
Meat & startch = gas
Melons are best eaten by themselves
Chocolate goes with anything *(Just kidding...not)*
Pineapple after a meal with help with digestion
Papaya is good for digestion too, although not everyone likes it.
Peppermint tea also helps digestion. It's really good with 1/2 tsp of honey

Why does proper digestion matter? Well, besides the obvious, unless food is properly
digested it can't be assimilated and used up by the body. Instead, its elements are stored
in unsightly fat cells or scooted out of the body entirely. They also cause one to emit
embarrassingly unfeminine sounds and foul odors (farting)

If your internal organs are making noises and causing discomfort as a routine
after meals, see your doctor or chiropractor. You might have a food allergy.

Eating Tip for Better Digestion

Don't eat when you are upset. Stress can interfere with your natural digestive process
causing "heartburn" or gas. Either way, it isn't attractive!

What's a doll to do? Starve? No, hon. Calm down first. Take a few deep breaths.
Concentrate on your breathing. Then eat.

You can think about "killing" (metaphorically) that bum later.
Imagine his head exploding like a fiery balloon,
bouncing back like rubber 'til his eyes bug out, then pop back in his head.
Oooh! That must have hurt. Heh, heh.
Watch it puffing up with the hot air you've known all along fills his head,
until he's so big you think he's going to pop again...can't wait, can you?
Then see him floating far, far away ~ way up in the sky ~ away from you
~ forgive, release it and forget/detach.

Now, feel like having dessert?

SPILLS & STAINS

Club soda

Wine, soy sauce to name two. Dab club soda on as soon as possible
with a clean cloth underneath. Press, never rub a stain.

Vinegar

Gets out many types of stains. Use sparingly and blot it out.
Try a mild solution of vinegar and water on a lace tablecloth.

Spilled eggs

Sponge up with cold water. It's not a good idea to reuse them.

Getting lipstick off your collar

Ha! You think I'm going to tell you?

Blood

Sprinkle talcum powder on the stain to dry, then brush away.
Soak fabric in cold water.
Pour detergent on stain and gently scrub sides of fabric together.
Rinse in cold water.
Don't use hot water as it will set the stain.

To bleach a blood stain, pour hydrogen peroxide over it.
Let it work for a minute, then wash fabric.
Note: Make sure your fabric is bleachable before using hydrogen peroxide.

Chewing gum

Put ice on it. When it freezes, chip it off.

To get gum out of hair, smother it in peanut butter or baby oil.
Rub it out of hair with your fingers. Have patience! It really works.

NATURAL PEST REPELLENTS
Most bugs don't like vitamin B

Taking B vitamins is a great way to ward off mosquitos, gnats and fleas. They seem to find the vitamin odor offensive. *Note: Those bugs seem to be the most attracted to people who eat a lot of sweets. Apparently, they don't find chocolate offensive. But, who does?*

If you get stung anyway, put some meat tenderizer or papaya on it. The papain enzyme helps to break down the poison and heal the sting. A baking soda salve also helps to absorb some of the venom. If you're roughing it, a dollop of cool mud will do the trick!

Protect your pets, too!
Give them pet-style brewer's yeast tablets for natural flea control.
Give them garlic for worms.

Bee stings

Cool mud will relieve pain from the sting from bees. As it dries, it absorbs the venom. Vitamin C helps the body heal faster from a sting. If you are allergic to bees, or puff up and have trouble breathing, seek medical attention immediately.

Ant trails

Pour baby powder as a barrier. The ants won't walk across the powder because it clings to their skin and dries them out. A chalk line around your pet's dish should keep them out of their food and water too. Diatomaceous earth is the best barrier.
As about it at your local nursery.

Ants don't like coffee grounds but the plants and flowers love them!
Throw your used grounds into the garden and around the base of your house,
to keep ants out. Watch your garden flourish!
Note: Ants don't like boiling water poured on them either.

Cedar

Keep moths out of your closet with cedar. Most drugstores have cedar blocks or balls you can hang in your closet or place in your dresser drawers.

Vinegar and water

Spray a mixture of equal parts vinegar and water on sinks and counter tops to keep ants away. It also kills some harmful bacteria that can grow on kitchen and bathroom surfaces.

How to Stretch Your Meal

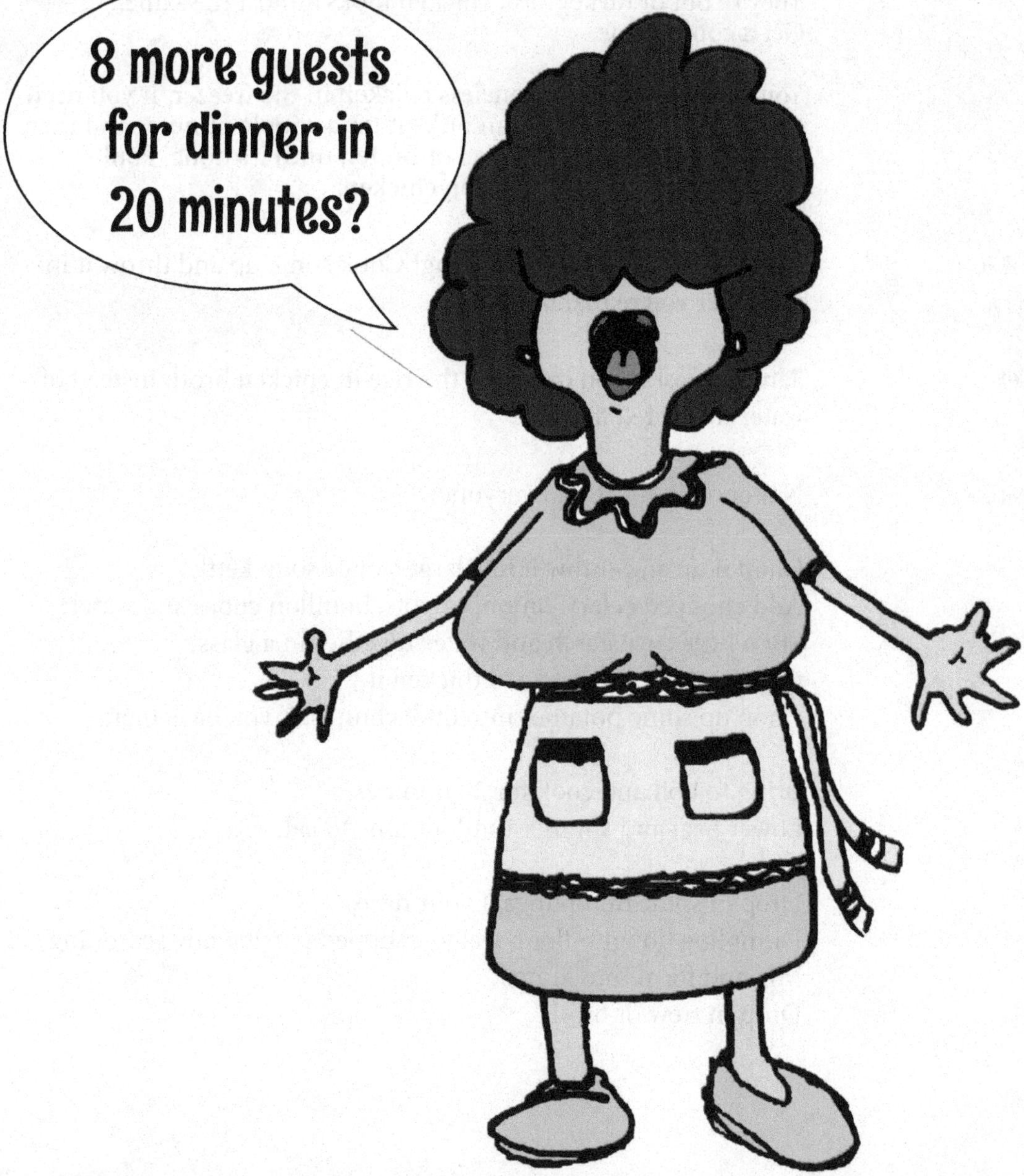

Last minute company? No problem!

HOW TO STRETCH YOUR MEAL

Meal type

Turkey -   Nobody cares about seeing a whole bird on a plate anyway. Cut it up this year. Rush to the deli counter. Pick up a hunk of unsliced real turkey. Pull it apart with a fork, throw it in a pan with a little watered-down gravy. Heat it up and add it to your platter.

They're out of turkey? Eh, chicken looks almost the same. Get a cooked one.

You might keep some boneless chicken in the freezer. If you need to use it in a hurry, you can nuke it for a couple minutes and then cook it in a pan with olive oil or butter, until it's done. Poultry seasoning or lemon is tasty on chicken.

Pasta -   Pasta goes with almost anything! Cook some up and throw it in whatever you're making.

Rice -   Same as pasta. You can cook the rice in chicken broth instead of water for added flavor.

Meat -   Not enough meat for everyone?

Chop it up and throw it in a large pot or soup kettle.
Add chopped celery, onion, carrots, bouillon cubes and water.
Stir a little cornstarch and water together in a glass,
then stir it into the stew to thicken it.
Chop up some potatoes into little chunks, if you have them.

Bring to boil and cook for 20 minutes.
Lower heat and simmer until it's time to eat.

Drop in some dumplings if your dare.
Dumpling dough - flour, water, chopped parsley, any seasoning.
Mix and form into lumps.
Drop in stew or broth.

Salad -

Add vegetables to your salad.
Chop the veggies into little cubes and chop the lettuce into bite size pieces. Add apple chunks, and/or blueberries, pomegranate seeds, even chunks of cheese.

Add croutons if you have them.
You can make croutons by toasting bread in the oven.
Both sides.
Season the bread with any flavor you like.
(Garlic and parmesan perhaps).

Before you add nuts, know your guests.
Make sure no one is allergic. When in doubt don't use.

Don't give strawberries to babies or young children unless you know they aren't allergic.

Snacks -

Let them fill up on chips and dip. They'll have less room for dinner.

Sidedish -

Cook something else!

Make a completely different dish from any ingredients you've got in the fridge or pantry.

Use leftovers from last night's dinner.
Serve a little of each dish to everyone at the table.

Don't explain.
They'll just think you couldn't make up your mind on what to serve.

Don't worry -   Last resort - or brilliant idea - ORDER DELIVERY!

Have a good time.

Enjoy your company, your family and friends. They are the reason you are getting together anyway. Remember, if the dinner is really bad, it will be a great conversation piece for your next party. The worse it is today, the funnier it will be tomorrow.

The Day After

THE DAY AFTER

What to do with those leftovers

Turkey - GREAT TURKEY SANDWICH! Smear mayonaisse on two slices of bread. Smother them with turkey. Add cheese if you'd like. Place under broiler until mayonaisse begins to bubble or cheese melts. Put both slices together. Indulge!

Fruit - SMOOTHIES! Throw your leftover fruit in a blender. Add rum and whirl!

Or - skip the booze and use protein powder and ice.

Pizza - Heat it up in the oven. Slice into squares and serve with a fun drink.

Salad Toppings - Great in omelettes, pasta and goulash (no lettuce)

Flowers - Cut blossoms off stems. Place blossoms on a cookie sheet in a single layer. Place in oven with pilot light. Do NOT turn oven on! Use a wad of aluminum foil to keep the oven door open a crack. Let the flowers dry overnight. Arrange potpourri in a bowl.

Options - Add sliced apples, oranges, whole cloves, allspice and cinnamon sticks. Sprinkle with extra cinnamon before drying. Add a few small pine cones to our potpourri for a wintery effect.

HOW TO GET OVER THAT FAT, DUMPY, LARD-FILLED DEPRESSED FEELING WE GET FROM EATING NACHOS AND HOT FUDGE SUNDAES THE NIGHT BEFORE

No guilt allowed!

If you're going to indulge yourself, enjoy it fully. Each day is special, unique.
You really can make up for it the day after.

I get myself in trouble diet-wise when I "deprive" myself. If I'm feeling restricted, I want more. When I'm told I can't do something, it becomes the thing I want to do most. So, when I wanted to lose weight, I stopped dieting and started concentrating on how foods made me feel after I ate them. I learned about their health content, what vitamins they had in them and tried to stay away from eating "empty calories." "Empty calories" is a name we've given foods that have very little nutritional value. You know, all the good stuff. Chocolate, sugar, cream puffs, potato chips, donuts, etc.

I started concentrating on me. I tossed out the bathroom scale and all my calorie counters. I began to focus on what made me happy, gave me comfort. What was it about food that I enjoyed the most? Why was food so important to me? Was it a replacement for something missing in my life?

Well, at first I got really depressed. I had dreams I was running down the frozen food aisle of the grocery store, stuffing my face with chocolate eclairs. Show's you how deprived I felt, I normally would have let them thaw before eating 'em.

Finally, I went to the health food store and read books about nutrition and healthful food combinations. I was amazed at how simple it was. Now, I don't limit myself. I limit the "funk food." Foods that make me feel in a "funk" after I eat them. I try to stay away from sugar, high fat dairy products, red meat and processed foods.

I found that although a quart of ice cream tastes fabulous going down, a parfait glass of fresh mixed berries and apples makes me feel better afterwards. Indulging in foods without a lot of fat and sugar gives me pep, makes me feel sexier, and gets rid of my zits... yes, doll, even at my age.

Of course, there are those days when nothin' but nachos will do it for me. I will then treat myself with the full knowledge of how I'll look, feel and fit into my jeans the day after...and I'll enjoy it none-the-less!

That's the secret. When you enjoy each day, do things that you want to do, eat what you want to eat, you don't want as much, because you have it all. You don't need to fill voids in your life, because there aren't any. If you decide you want to change something about yourself, do it for you. For how a healthful lifestyle will make you feel both physically and mentally.

Add nutritious foods to your meals. I try to throw extra veggies into everything. Pile them on! I get so full and satisfied over the blend of flavors and amount of food, that most of the time, I don't even want dessert. Well unless my husband asks me...you know how they get that look iin their eyes, kinda sway their heads back and forth, and say in that really, low, smooth voice..."how about some dessert, baby?" The first time you see it, you laugh your head off. But, afterwards, you're glad that you didn't eat so much you have to unzip your pants and lay down in the back of the stationwagon on the way home from the restaurant.

Remember, you're in control. When you don't feel guilty and don't deprive yourself, you don't want as much anyway. *And if anybody picks on you, flip 'em off with a smile!*

Anyway, here are a few tricks for "cleaning out" the day after:

Lemon and water -   Squeeze half a lemon into a glass of water. It cuts the mucus in your throat. Some say it helps to cleanse the liver, too.

Walk in the garden -   Great for cleansing the mind. Look at the birds, trees and flowers. Don't think. Just observe.

They say that bluebirds bring happiness. Don't stand under one for too long, though, or they'll give you a little more than you wanted, on the shoulder of your favorite shirt.

A smelly brew -   A clove of garlic (chopped), 1 Tbsp of fresh chopped parsley, 2 Tbsp of apple cider vinegar, in 8 oz of water. Drink it...sip if you'd like over time. It helps to cleanse the system and ward off cold and flu bugs. If you drink too much of it, it will ward your friends off, too.

Take a bath -

Or a shower. Scrub your skin gently with a loofah or bath brush to remove dead skin cells. Wash your hair, do your grooming, give yourself a facial.

Exercise -

I know, everybody says to exercise. It really does make you feel good (after). Start slow, a little at a time. Baby steps. Be gentle with yourself - and Breathe! Taking deep, relaxed breaths when exercising can help to release some toxins in your system. If you use weights, breathe out on the hard stuff, in on the release. Then stretch afterwards, and make circle movements a couple of times with your arms, legs to balance your qi.

Vitamins & Herbs -

There are many good vitamin supplements and herbal remedies on the market. Consult with your doctor or chiropractor on which health supplements are the best for you. Bodies are different and have varying needs, so find out what your body needs and if you are allergic to anything from an expert. Also, don't overdo vitamins. More is not necessarily better. Best to follow directions.

Eat -

Intermittent fasting is good sometimes but to keep your metabolism up to give you energy to stay strong during the day, we need to eat. There is so much advice on how and what to eat, do what you decide is best for you.

Perhaps, keep it simple...don't eat empty calories (foods with little or no nutritional value) and try to avoid processed foods. If you are going to eat sugar etc, own it.

Do it without guilt.

Then eat more nutritionally. If you can go for 3 or more days without sugar, your body may stop craving sugar.

Remember, you are what you eat. feed your body well and it will respond nicely for you.

FOR THE BOD

Ready - To - Wear - Foods

Banana

Wet hair. Mash banana and spread on ends of hair. Leave on for 15 minutes,
then wash hair. It makes a great pre-conditioner for softer hair!

Mayonnaise

Softens dry hair! Rub about 2 Tbsp mayonnaise ito the hair. Leave on for about 15 minutes.
Then, shampoo as you normally do.

Avocado

Facial mask. Moisturizing. The vitamin A in the avocado is good for the skin, too.
Mush into hair. Leave on for 5 minutes. Scrape off with tortilla chips - just kidding.
Wash off with shampoo. Rinse.

Egg White

Facial mask. Toner. Beat egg white gently, spread on face in upward strokes.
Leave on for about 20 minutes. It will tighten up. Whatever you do, don't answer the door!

Honey

To diminish blackheads, heat honey slightly, not too hot, and pat onto face.
After a few minutes wash off with warm water.

Option: Add a small amount of honey to beaten egg whites. Give it a good stir and then pat
onto face. Leave on for about 20 minutes.
Wash with a good facial cleanser while gently scrubbing with a loofah.
Note: This mixture will remain sticky.
Don't lay your face on anything you'd rather not carry with you while you're wearing it.

Plain Yogurt

Apply to face. Semi-moisturizing. Acidophilus cultures are good for the skin.

Papaya

Apply mashed papaya to face. It softens and removes dead skin cells. Make sure the papaya isn't too ripe though. Fermented (too ripe) papaya may make your skin red. T
est a little on your or your friend's forearm first. lol.
When you use a papaya mask, leave it on for about 15 to 20 minutes, then wash off.

Eating papaya is good for digestion. Some people like it with a squeeze of fresh lime.

Cucumber

Place cucumber slices on your eyelids to reduce puffiness and brighten the eyes.
It will cause your eyes to tear a little bit. Remove your eye makeup first.
Lay down and elevate your feet on pillows or against the wall. Relax for 15 minutes,
then wash your face with cold water, finishing with cold water.

Lemon

One half of a lemon, squeezed into a large glass of water is a fabulous cleansing drink.
They say it's good for the liver.
It's also good on the elbows to remove dead flaky skin.

Distilled Water & Aloe Vera Spritz

Fill a mist bottle with filtered or distilled water. Add 3 Tbsp. pure aloe vera get.
Shake. Mist your face during the day. It freshens - even over makeup.

Teabags

Reduces puffiness around the eyes. Steep them for a minute, then press the hot water out.
When cool enough, place one on each eyelid. Relax for 10 minutes.
Remove the teabags. Splash your face with cool water.

Bentonite

Bentonite is volcanic ash. You can buy it at most health food stores or online. It is like a clay.
Mix a little of it in a dish with cold water. Spread on your skin. It pulls toxins from your
skin. You can add it to bath water too if you'd like. Too much might clog drains as it is
like mud when mixed with water. It works nicely though. Use paper towels to remove the
clumps from your skin and toss them in the trash. Rinse the rest off with warm water and
follow with a cold water rinse. Moisturize with a natural organic lotion, oil or serum. Or
follow with an egg or yogurt facial to feed your skin, and then moisturize.

Papaya

Apply mashed papaya to face. It softens and removes dead skin cells. Make sure the papaya isn't too ripe though. Fermented (too ripe) papaya may make your skin red. T
est a little on your or your friend's forearm first. lol.
When you use a papaya mask, leave it on for about 15 to 20 minutes, then wash off.

Eating papaya is good for digestion. Some people like it with a squeeze of fresh lime.

Cucumber

Place cucumber slices on your eyelids to reduce puffiness and brighten the eyes.
It will cause your eyes to tear a little bit. Remove your eye makeup first.
Lay down and elevate your feet on pillows or against the wall. Relax for 15 minutes,
then wash your face with cold water, finishing with cold water.

Lemon

One half of a lemon, squeezed into a large glass of water is a fabulous cleansing drink.
They say it's good for the liver.
It's also good on the elbows to remove dead flaky skin.

Distilled Water & Aloe Vera Spritz

Fill a mist bottle with filtered or distilled water. Add 3 Tbsp. pure aloe vera get.
Shake. Mist your face during the day. It freshens - even over makeup.

Teabags

Reduces puffiness around the eyes. Steep them for a minute, then press the hot water out.
When cool enough, place one on each eyelid. Relax for 10 minutes.
Remove the teabags. Splash your face with cool water.

Bentonite

Bentonite is volcanic ash. You can buy it at most health food stores or online. It is like a clay.
Mix a little of it in a dish with cold water. Spread on your skin. It pulls toxins from your
skin. You can add it to bath water too if you'd like. Too much might clog drains as it is
like mud when mixed with water. It works nicely though. Use paper towels to remove the
clumps from your skin and toss them in the trash. Rinse the rest off with warm water and
follow with a cold water rinse. Moisturize with a natural organic lotion, oil or serum. Or
follow with an egg or yogurt facial to feed your skin, and then moisturize.

BEAUTIFUL BATHING

There are so many wonderful products on the market.
Add fun and fragrance to your baths and showers.
Some products can help you to feel better too!

Aromatic Oils

Pour a few drops of aromatic oil into your bath water as the tub begins to fill.
Read the descriptions and choose the oils best for you.

Bubble Bath

These days, there are so many types to choose from you'll be able to
find the perfect bubbles for your every mood.

Baking Soda

Add a few tablespoons of baking soda to your bath. It pulls some toxins from your skin.

Candles

Light candles in safe places away from your hair and other flammable things, or use the
faux ones. Play soft music and turn the lights down. Add bubbles to your bath and soak
your stress away. Adding a companion is fun too.

Tea

You can add a few herbal tea bags to your bath water instead of aromatic oils.
Camomile for relieving tension. Peppermint or spearmint to perk you up. Comfrey to help
minor aches feel better. If you make your bath water too strong, you might want to shower
afterwards to get the tea off. Don't drink the water...

Mineral Salts

If you're feeling a bit depleted or have minor aches and pains, a mineral bath might be the
perfect thing to energize you. Shop for bath therapies or salts (epsom salts).
Don't soak too long - prune fingers aren't pretty.

Bath Buddies

These are always fun.

FANTASY DINNERS

Let them cook for you

Creating together

Making dishes together can be fun.
Or instead of chopping, stirring, and cooking,
use all that energy on each other and go for the delivery option.

Delivery

Pick out the flyers from our favorite restaurants.
Let them choose the food to be delivered.
Hop back into the jacuzzi until your meal arrives.

For Dad

There are other ways to cook besides bar-b-que

OUR DAD
was the inspiration for our book

Recently divorced after 30 years of marriage - So, it was to three wives, who's counting?
He's now out on his own, angain.

For a very special dinner, he decided to cook lobster tails.
He got the butter out, melted it perfectly, placed the lobster tails in the oven,
set it on broil - then went upstairs to take a shower!

Several minutes pass. Smoke begins to fill the kitchen. Hmm! He's thinking...
something smells awfully good. The neighbors must be bar-b-queing.

Smoke alarms go off. OH NO! The patter of little wet feet are heard running to the kitchen.
The oven door swings open - then, CLANG! Thud. Aou! Aou! Aou!

Needless to say, he went out for dinner that evening.

We bought him a new pan and oven mitts for Christmas.

HEY DAD!

Here's a section just for you!

How to Boil Water

Fill a pot with cold water and place it on the stove. Turn the burner under the pot on high. After a few minutes, the water will start to bubble. Let it boil for at least one minute. This will ge rid of any bacteria or chemical residue in the water. Then, reduce the heat and add whatever you are going to make.

If you ever have to boil drinking water after a flood or something, boil it longer - like 5 to 10 minutes. Then strain it through a cotton shirt or cheesecloth to get rid of dirt and stuff.

Tip from Flo: If you have a gas stove, make sure the burner is lit. If it won't light, check the pilot light. Wait for any gas to dissipate before re-lighting the pilot. You don't need to lean over and watch it light closely. Keep your head and sleeves away from the stove, just in case.

How To Make Tea or Cocoa In The Microwave

Fill a cup with water.
Make sure there is no metal anywhere on the cup. Metal makes a microwave blow up.
Nuke the cup on high for one minute. Use a pot holder to remove the cup from the microwave as it might be hot. Add a tea bag or cocoa mix to the water and stir.
For yummy cocoa add marshmallows.

How To Make Tea or Cocoa Without A Microwave

Look for the tea kettle. It may be on the stove or in a cupboard. Fill it with water.
(you don't have to fill it all the way up, just enough to make the drinks.)
Turn the stove on to the highest setting. Place the tea kettle on the stove.
It will either whistle or blow steam out of its spout when the water is hot.
Fill a cup with hot water and add flavorings.

Corn On The Cob

Peel and discard the husk and stringy things. Wrap the cob in two paper towels, making sure the entire ear of corn is covered. Run it under the faucet to get it wet. Place it in the microwave and nuke on high for about 11 minutes.

Serve with those cute little corn holders. Use butter or yogurt for flavoring if you need it.

Dad's favorite corn flavoring: Roll corn in plain yogurt and parmesan cheese. Mmm!

Baked Potatoes

Gently scrub and rinse the potatoes. Wrap each potato in paper towels, covering them entirely. Get the paper towels a little wet, but not soaked.

Place the potatoes in the microwave (no more than two at a time) and nuke on high for about 5 minutes. After 5 minutes, turn them and cook them for 5 more minutes.
Let stand for 3 minutes.

Use a pot holder to remove them from the oven. Squeeze each one gently to check if they are done. They should give just a little and be soft in the middle.
Wrap in towel or potholder to keep warm until you serve.

For fluffy potatoes, microwave them until they are almost done and then pop them in a pre-heated oven (set at 425) for about 10 minutes.
The skin should be crispy and the insides should be fluffy.

Optional garnishes:
    Butter
    Parmesan cheese
    Sour cream
    Yogurt
    Chives
    Chopped onions
    Cheese
    Broccoli

Twice Baked Potatoes

Potatoes
Milk
Butter
Seasoning
Green onion (diced)
Cheddar cheese (grated)

Cook the potatoes as suggested in the recipe on the previous page. Cut a long slit in each potato and spoon the insides into a bowl.

Add a little milk, butter, seasoning, chopped green onion or chives and mash it up. You can use a mixer if you want.

Spoon the mixture back into the potato skins and top with cheese. Place them on a microwaveable dish and nuke for a minute or so until the cheese is melted. Garnish immediately with diced green onion or chives.

Cindy's BBQ Chicken

3/4 cup orange juice
6 Tbsp. honey
6 Tbsp mustard
2 tsp fresh chopped rosemary
Boneless skinless chicken meat

Mix the ingredients together in a pan. Marinate overnight in the fridge. Barbque to perfection the next day. Incredibly delicious!

Frozen Entrees

Frozen dinner (your favorite)
Frozen side dishes (vegetables)
2 quarts water
Garnish

Hide the packages and no one will know you didn't make this meal from scratch!
(Unless they have the recipe too!)

Fill a sauce pan with water and bring to a boil.

With a knife, carefully slit the end of the box containing pouches of frozen side dishes. DO NOT PIERCE THE POUCHES.

Slowly slide the pouches into the boiling water The watter will automatically cool to a simmer. When it returns to boil, lower the heat and simmer for about 5 minutes.

While that's cooking, open the box containing the frozen entree. Slit a small hole in the plastic wrap and pop that baby in the microwave. Read the package for heat level and cooking duration.

When your side dishes are cooked, remove the plastic pouches from the hot water with a fork or tongs. Place them on a flat surface (a plate will do nicely). Slit the pouch on the side that is away from you (unless of course, you'd like to steam your face). Then, up end it and let the contents slide onto your plate or serving platter.

Repeat the process until all the side dish pouches are empty.

Remove the entree from the microwave and arrange the contents on a plate or platter. Garnish with parsley or twisted orange.

Dinner For Two

2 artichokes
Steamed vegetables
Filets of fish
Pumpernickel rolls

Broccoli tops (they look like little green bouquets)
1/2 cup onion (diced)
Zucchini (sliced)
Yellow squash (sliced)
Green bell pepper (chop strips in half)
Red bell pepper (chop strips in half)
Butter
Mayonaisse

Get a big pot and fill it with about 3 inches of water. Place a colander inside the pot.

Wash the artichokes and cut off their stems at the base of the leaves. Place them on the colander. For an added flair you can snip off the sharp point on each leaf with scissors. Place the lid on the top of the pot.

Turn the stove on medium high. The water will start to boil. Check the water level in 15 minute. Cook these for 45 minutes. Add more water if necessary so the pot doesn't burn.

The artichokes are done when their leaves can be pulled off easily. *(They are overdone when they fall apart, but are also very good that way.)*

If you don't have a collander you can cook the artichokes in water. Just let them bob up and down. Steaming them leaves more vitamins in the artichokes, but you don't have to use a collander.

You have about 15 minutes until you need to prepare the fish and veggies. You can mix a drink, take a quick shower or arrange some flowers for the table.

About 15 minutes before the artichokes are ready (30 minutes of cooking) get out the sliced / cut vegetables you picked up from the store.

Place these vegetables inside a second collander or in a second pot, filled with some water.

Add 2 filets of fish on top of the veggies.

Dinner For Two (continued)

Place this collander on top of the artichokes collander or place it in a second pot of water. Make sure the water level is below the veggies. If you are just using a pot, add about an inch of water. Make sure the water doesn't all evaporate, add more if necessary. When the water evaporates while you are cooking your pan could burn and this changes the flavor of your food.

It only takes about 5 to 10 minutes to cook the fish. Sprinkle the fish with lemon or with your favorite seasoning. Garlic or Mrs. Dash work nicely.

Melt butter to dip the artichoke leaves in. Mayonaisse is good for dipping too.

Place the veggies on a plate. Add the fish on top of that. The fish should be flaky when touched with a fork. Garnish with lemon. Serve as soon as the artichokes are done. Place the artichokes in bowls. Have a plate or bowl handy for discarding the eaten artichoke leaves.

Barbecued Veggies

Yellow and green zucchini
Mushrooms
Bell peppers (Yellow, Red, Green)
Pearl onions (peeled or canned & drained)
Olive Oil
Garlic
Herbs (Rosemary, Italian blend, or your favorite seasoning)

Chop vegetables into chunks and place on foil. Sprinkle a little oil on top. Add garlic and seasoning. Wrap up tightly and cook on the barbeque. Turn frequently to prevent burning.

Or

Bake in oven for 10 minutes.

Shrimp Kabobs

Shrimp
Pineapple chunks
Onion chunks
Bell pepper chunks
Low salt soy sauce or teriyaki sauce
Lemon juice
3 Tbsp. grated ginger
1/4 cup honey

Option: Substitute steak, chicken or eggplant for shrimp

Alternate the shrimp, pineapple, onion and bell pepper on skewers. Lay in some type of pan.

Mix soy or teriyaki sauce, juice from lemon, ginger and honey together, then sprinkle it on the meat/eggplant.

Marinate for 30 minutes in the fridge.

Barbeque until done. Serve over cooked rice or noodles.

Option: pour chicken broth into pot. Add diced green onions. Bring to boil. Serve with kabobs and rice or noodles.

Barbequed Clams

Live little neck clams
1/2 cup butter
2 Tbsp garlic
2 cups clam juice
1 tsp lemon juice
Crusty bread

Place butter, garlic, lemon and clam juices in metal pan. Make sure the handle is metal too. Have an oven mitt handy.

Melt butter mixture at back of barbeque grill.

Cook clams on grill until they open. If they don't open, don't eat them.

Skewer the meat with a long toothpick or wooden skewer Dip in butter mixture. Cook more clams.

Take a piece of crust bread and OH NO! You dropped it in the butter mixture! Well, don't let it go to waste! Yum!

Teriyaki Tuna

Fresh Ahi tuna
1 onion (sliced)
1 red bell pepper (sliced)
1 orange or yellow bell pepper (sliced)
Mushrooms (sliced)
Lemon
Teriyaki sauce
Fresh ginger

Cut tuna into steaks.
Slice vegetables.
Place tuna steaks and vegetables in a dish. Pour teriyaki sauce on top and squeeze lemon over it all. Grate fresh ginger and place all around.

Cover and refrigerate for about 15 minutes. Barbeque tuna until done.
Cook vegetables in foil or a pan on the grill. Serve together.

Option: Roll tuna steaks in coarsely ground pepper and sear over fire for five minutes or until done. They should be slightly uncooked in the center. Slice into thin pieces and serve over salad.

Beach Bake

Cook at the beach while you play in the surf.
Bake your bod and dinner at the same time!

Dig -
Find a good spot on the beach where it's legal to have a fire.
Dig a hole in the sand 3 to 4 feet deep.
Line it with oak or other hardwood.
Lay rocks around the wood.
Light a big fire and let it burn for 1 to 4 hours while you sunbathe and swim.
(Leave someone to watch the firepit so no one falls into it.)

Bake -
After the fire subsides, the rocks will be very hot.
Lay seaweed on the rocks and cover it with gauze or an old towel.
Wrap your food securely in aluminum foil - unless you like the taste of sand in your food.
Lay your food in a towel on the seaweed.
Drip a little seawater on the towel to create steam.
Cover it with sand or a heavy tarp and let it bake for about an hour.
About 15 minutes before you eat, toss a foil wrapped loaf of crusty bread in to warm it up.

Good foods to cook this way are:
Clams
Seafood
Shellfish
Chicken (pre-cooked)*
Corn on the cob
Potatoes
Vegetables braised with oil and garlic.
Balsamic vinegar and olive oil with garlic makes a nice dip for bread and veggies.

*We pre-cook the chicken until its almost done at home,
then beach bake it the rest of the way for added flavor.*

After about an hour, dig out your dinner.
Remember it may be hot. Might be a good idea to use a mitt to unwrap it.

Snuggle under a blanket and nibble on your lobster
while you gaze at the setting sun on the horizon.

Life is fun, isn't it?

Index

Made in the USA
Columbia, SC
25 November 2024

46736019R00111